The *Ultimate* *Betrayal*

A Renewed Look at Intimate Partner Violence

Tricia B. Bent-Goodley

NASW PRESS
National Association of Social Workers
Washington, DC

Jeane W. Anastas, PhD, LMSW, President
Elizabeth J. Clark, PhD, ACSW, MPH, Executive Director

Cheryl Y. Bradley, *Publisher*
Lisa M. O'Hearn, *Managing Editor*
Sarah Lowman, *Project Manager*
Kathleen P. Baker, *Copyeditor*
Rebecca Tippets, *Proofreader*
Karen Schmitt, *Indexer*

Cover by Naylor Design, Inc.
Interior design by Rick Soldin
Printed and bound by Sheridan Books, Inc.

First impression: August 2011

Library of Congress Cataloging-in-Publication Data

Bent-Goodley, Tricia B.
  The ultimate betrayal : a renewed look at intimate partner violence / Tricia
B. Bent-Goodley.
      p. cm.
  Includes bibliographical references and index.
  ISBN 978-0-87101-418-4
362.   Intimate partner violence. I. Title.
  HV6626.B45 2011
  362.82'92—dc22

                                                              2010047787

Printed in the United States of America

This book is dedicated to my husband, Marvin D. Goodley, and my sons
Malcolm and Marcus Goodley

In Memoriam
Willie James Swain
Bermel Bent
Carolyn Falconer

Contents

Acknowledgments

I am first grateful to God for giving me a chance to invest my time and energy in doing work that is so important to me. I am particularly thankful to my editor, Lisa O'Hearn, who was so patient and understanding as she waited to receive the manuscript. Thanks to the NASW staff for all of their hard work and commitment to producing this book. My students at Howard University are simply amazing. I decided to write this book during a class on domestic violence with my students. I also have the best graduate assistants. I want to particularly thank Paulette Hubbert, Damien Frierson, and April Ivey who helped me with completing tasks for the book. I marvel at the resilience and strength of the survivors whom I have served as a professional social worker. I hope this book will provide other practitioners with what they need to better support and assist them.

I am fortunate to have a wonderful circle of family and friends who support me, and I appreciate their patience with me. I am also blessed to have mentors to advise and guide me. I am especially thankful to Dr. Iris Carlton-LaNey, Dr. Lawrence Gary, and Dr. King Davis. I especially thank them for their investment in my personal and professional development. I am thankful for having two parents who gave so much of themselves to support me and brothers and sisters who have supported me throughout my life. My husband and boys are my greatest joy and anchor. Finally, I appreciate the ancestors who paved a way for me to do what I do each day. I hope I can do the same for others on their journey.

Thank you to my sisters of Alpha Kappa Alpha Sorority, Howard University Women As Change Agents, and all of my sisters in service.

About the Author

Tricia B. Bent-Goodley, PhD, is professor of social work at Howard University. Dr. Bent-Goodley has a passion for creating solutions to improve the safety and viability of families, with a particular focus on the development of culturally specific faith- and community-based interventions that strengthen families and communities of color. She is the author or coauthor of three books in the area of social policy. Dr. Bent-Goodley serves in a number of local, state, and nationally elected and appointed leadership positions, for example, as a member of the Prince George's County Domestic Violence Fatality Review; member of the National Association of Social Workers Committee on the Role and Status of Women; Steering Committee member of the Institute on Domestic Violence in the African American Community; and cochair of the NABSW National Academy for African-Centered Social Work. Before coming to Howard University, she served as an administrator and clinical practitioner in the area of family violence, school, and community practice. Dr. Bent-Goodley received her PhD in social work with specialization in social policy, planning, and analysis from Columbia University; her master's degree in social work from the University of Pennsylvania; and her bachelor of arts degree in sociology from Queens College of the City University of New York. Dr. Bent-Goodley finds her greatest joy in being a wife and a mother of two boys.

One

Overview of Intimate Partner Violence

Domestic violence is a serious problem that affects countless people, families, and communities across this nation and around the world. No specific visual representation of a survivor or perpetrator of abuse exists, which makes this issue challenging to address. The idea of the ultimate betrayal speaks to the multiple violations of trust that often occur in domestic violence situations. These levels of trust are at the individual, familial, communal, and societal levels. At the individual level, the woman may feel that she has betrayed herself by not recognizing the signs, being in the situation, rationalizing the violence, or not leaving the abuser. In many ways, the woman has to learn how to trust herself again, and so domestic violence goes beyond the violent incident and speaks largely to being able to trust oneself and others again. Also, she may be in denial of the abuse and overlook the violence because she values the relationship she thought she had or because she is afraid to leave the relationship. Betrayal occurs at the relationship level because the perpetrator presents himself as a partner, which should mean that love, care, and respect are present. When the woman finds that these are missing, she feels a sense of betrayal because the perpetrator is not who he portrayed himself to be. This sense of betrayal also occurs at the community level because community members often choose not to get involved or promote staying in the relationship at the woman's expense. These actions condone the abuse. Betrayal at the societal level occurs because systems continue to be unresponsive and ineffective and lack understanding of domestic violence. Therefore, multiple violations of the layers of trust occur that can become lethal for far too many women.

This book is written not just for professional social workers, but also for people who are trying to find answers related to domestic violence and how they can better respond to this problem. In this book, I present current knowledge and information about intimate partner violence and provide a safe place to examine yourself, your thoughts, and your experiences and how they have affected your perceptions, your attitudes, and your actions or inaction. Consider this book a conversation between the two of us that will allow you to develop an action plan to strengthen your response to this issue. I integrate discussion of cultural context into the book because issues of diversity cannot be separated from the realities of domestic violence. An opportunity for reflection on each issue is presented at the end of each chapter. I understand that people can know the definition of "domestic violence," understand the cycle of abuse, and even know the theories of what causes domestic violence but still have attitudes and beliefs that render them ineffective at being helpful. I have also found that even when the survivor is no longer in the relationship, she still experiences the impact of the abuse. At community trainings and professional workshops, someone will have the courage to say, "I went through this," "I survived," "I'm healing," or "I'm still on the journey of trying to heal." Being able to understand this issue and explore its relevance to you is vital. The Reflecting Pool is an opportunity for you to explore your thinking and identify where your attitude comes from and how you can further your thinking and perspective in a safe, nonthreatening place. Understanding domestic violence requires continual learning. The more you feel you know, the more you realize that there is more to learn and that your understanding of this issue can grow and evolve. At the end of each chapter, I provide resources relevant to that chapter that you can use to further your understanding, self-exploration, and knowledge.

Scope of the Problem

Domestic violence is a serious problem that affects people regardless of gender, race, ethnicity, religion, geographic location, income, class, education, age, or sexual orientation (Tjaden & Thoennes, 2000). No group is exempt from domestic violence. The challenges that face women globally with respect to violence are daunting. One-third of women across the globe have experienced some form of physical or sexual abuse over the course of their lifetime, and in most cases the perpetrator is someone in their own family (United Nations Development Fund for Women, 2003). Annually, between 40 percent and 70 percent of murdered women around the globe are killed by their partner (Garcia-Moreno, Jansen, Ellsberg, Heise, & Watts, 2005). One-third of women in the global community have experienced sexual, physical, or emotional abuse by an intimate partner over the course of their lifetime. Between 10 percent and nearly 70 percent of women have experienced some form of physical violence at the hands of an intimate partner, based on country-to-country comparisons. Women around the world continue to not be allowed to own property, possess money, dress as they choose, participate in decision making, or choose not to have sexual relations with their partner despite the risks of sexually transmitted infections and HIV (Chesler, 2009; Fontes & McCloskey, 2011; Garcia-Moreno et al., 2005). Understanding the global context of women's lives is important to understanding the prevalence of violence that they experience in their homes and the institutional structures that support women's disenfranchisement. One cannot separate violence experienced outside of the home from the risk of violence that women experience in their intimate relationships. So, although this book is specific to understanding violence as it relates to women in the United States, it is also important to understand the violence that women experience across the globe because they are connected.

In the United States, a woman is physically abused by her intimate partner every nine seconds. Nearly one-quarter of all U.S. women have experienced some form of abuse by an intimate partner (Centers for Disease Control and Prevention [CDC], 2008), with nearly one-third (31 percent) having been physically or sexually assaulted over the course of their lifetime (Commonwealth Fund, 1999). According to the National Crime

Victimization Survey, 691,710 nonfatal violent victimizations were committed by current or former spouses, boyfriends, or girlfriends of victims during 2000 (Rennison, 2003), most of which involved male perpetrators and female victims (Rennison, 2003; Smith & Farole, 2009). Yet, according to a CDC study on health care and domestic violence, an estimated 5 million women experience domestic violence each year (National Center for Injury Prevention and Control, 2003). Providers serve more than 65,000 women and children, with more than 9,000 calls to emergency hotlines daily going unanswered because of limited funding (National Network to End Domestic Violence, 2009). Young women between the ages of 16 and 24 are at the greatest risk for experiencing physical and sexual abuse (Rennison & Welchans, 2002). In a survey of 16,000 participants, 25 percent of women and nearly 8 percent of men were raped or physically abused by an intimate partner (Tjaden & Thoennes, 2000). Women are more likely to be stalked over the course of their lifetime and are more likely to know the stalker than are men. One in 12 women is estimated to experience stalking over the course of her lifetime compared with one in 45 men (Tjaden & Thoennes, 2000). Women are also more likely to be sexually assaulted over the course of their lifetime, with 78 percent of rape and sexual assault victims being women (Tjaden & Thoennes, 2000). Most victims (86 percent) of dating violence are female, and more than three women a day are murdered by an intimate partner (Catalano, 2007).

Income and employment play a factor; those in severe poverty and those who are unemployed are at the greatest risk of experiencing domestic violence (Goodwin, Chandler, & Meisel, 2003). Poor women are often more socially isolated, lack structural supports, have fewer viable networks to support them, and are geographically located in areas with limited resources (Levendosky et al., 2004; Trotter & Allen, 2009; Williams & Mickelson, 2004). In fact, domestic violence has been identified as the primary cause of homelessness for 44 percent of domestic violence survivors, and 33 percent of survivors have been homeless at least once as the result of trying to escape abuse (Baker, Cook, & Norris, 2003; U.S. Conference of Mayors, 2003).

Death by an Intimate Partner

Death by an intimate partner accounts for one-third (33 percent) of murdered women (Rennison, 2003). On average, more than three women are murdered by an intimate partner each day in the United States. Half of men in state prisons for a domestic violence offense killed their partner (Durose et al., 2005). In 2005, 1,510 people were killed by an intimate partner, with 78 percent of victims being women and 22 percent of victims being men (U. S. Department of Justice, 2009). Even among those men killed by an intimate partner, between 70 percent and 80 percent had a history of committing domestic violence against their partner before being killed (Campbell et al., 2003). One-fifth of women killed by an intimate partner had no initial sign of the abuse and were killed in the first physical incident of violence (Block, 2003). Most women are at greatest risk when they leave the relationship, with nearly one-half of murdered victims of intimate partner violence having just left the abuser (Block, 2003). Gun violence increases the risk of femicide by five times and is a major risk factor (Campbell et al., 2003). Of all women killed by a firearm, two-thirds were killed by an intimate partner (Violence Policy Center, 2004). In cases of murder-suicide or familicide (when the perpetrator also kills the children), a life-changing event such as job loss usually precedes the violence. The media often highlight these cases; however, murder–suicides are very rare and are typically committed by white, non-Hispanic men (Logan, Shannon, Walker, & Faragher, 2006). Regardless of how often familicide occurs, it is important to note that most of the men have been reported to law enforcement for domestic violence, so a prior history of abuse exists; having access to a gun increases the risk of lethality; the men often forecast what they are going to do by making very specific threats; and the use of drugs and alcohol, particularly alcohol, furthers the risk of abuse (Adams, 2007; Campbell, Glass, Sharps, Laughon, & Bloom, 2007; Rand & Saltzman, 2003; Smith & Farole, 2009).

Men as Victims of Intimate Partner Violence

Although discussion of men as victims of domestic violence by female perpetrators has been increasing, most incidents of intimate partner violence occur between a female survivor and a male perpetrator (Rennison, 2003). This fact does not devalue the experiences of men who experience abuse. All violence is wrong, whether the perpetrator is male or female, and systems need to be strengthened to serve all survivors and hold all perpetrators accountable, regardless of gender. To keep this issue in context, in 2003 intimate partner violence was identified in 20 percent of crimes committed against women and 3 percent of crimes committed against men. Women are the survivors of male-perpetrated intimate partner violence in 85 percent or more of cases of intimate partner violence (Rennison, 2003). Women are more likely than men to experience a physical injury as a result of a violent incident with an intimate partner, and women are more likely than men to sustain a physical injury as a result of domestic violence—nearly 40 percent of cases for women compared with 25 percent of cases for men. In terms of lifetime prevalence of violence, 25 percent of women older than age 18 have experienced some form of intimate partner victimization over the course of their lives compared with 7.6 percent of men. These numbers also have to be viewed in context. Much of the data that have been collected to examine the perpetration of violence among intimate partners does not identify cases in which the victim is reacting to long-term abuse or protecting himself or herself from ongoing violence. This lack of information does not allow researchers to capture these dynamics, and so although they have knowledge that men who are survivors of female-perpetrated intimate partner violence exist, they also recognize the importance of further inquiry with more specialized tools that identify the context in which the violence is being experienced. I still stress that violence is wrong regardless of the gender of the survivor, and we must ensure that systems are in place to respond to both men and women.

Older Adults and Intimate Partner Violence

A study conducted for the National Center on Elder Abuse (Otto & Quinn, 2007) found that 20 percent of reports of abuse of people older than age 60 were the result of domestic violence. The Administration on Aging

(2007) has estimated that a half-million older adults experience some form of domestic violence. Although being 16 to 24 years old is a risk factor for domestic violence, older women are also at grave risk. Older women often report more experiences of emotional abuse by partners and fewer experiences of physical abuse even when it occurs (Grossman & Lundy, 2003; Lundy & Grossman, 2009; Wilke & Vinton, 2005). Domestic violence is experienced in both long-term relationships and new relationships (Leisey, Kupstas, & Cooper, 2009; Lundy & Grossman, 2004; Straka & Montminy, 2006). Older women are faced with the complex issue of potentially dealing with 25, 30, or more years of marriage, which makes an important difference in their perceived options (Leisey et al., 2009). Older women also experience ageism; providers may not identify the risk of domestic violence or view incidents as domestic violence in older couples' relationships as readily as in younger couples' relationships. Older women are also more likely to have a disability and to be isolated as a result of the death of relatives and friends. One study found that older women were reluctant to seek help from formal providers and more likely to turn to family and the church for support (Beaulaurier, Seff, Newman, & Dunlop, 2007). More training is needed to learn how to better engage and support this population and explore policies and practices that can best assist them (Kilbane & Spira, 2010; Otto & Quinn, 2007). Intimate partner violence can no longer be viewed as an issue only for younger people.

Disabilities and Domestic Violence

The connection between disabilities and domestic violence has received increased attention. Women with disabilities tend to have a longer duration of abuse, which has been attributed, in part, to program inaccessibility and lack of structural supports such as interpreter services. This population experiences heightened risk because of the stigma associated with having a disability and potentially because they rely on the partner for personal and medical care, use of equipment, and transportation (Baladerian, 2009; Nixon, 2009). This imbalance of power is already present in the relationship, and so multiple layers of oppression need to be addressed. In fact, researchers are still trying to better identify the scope of this intersection, particularly among people of color and poor people, who are disproportionately more likely to struggle with this issue (Lightfoot & Williams, 2009; Mays, 2006). Women with disabilities are less likely to report verbal abuse and more likely to report physical abuse than they are other forms of violence (Slayter, 2009). More collaboration is needed among advocates working to end domestic violence, service providers, law enforcement, and court officers to better address this issue (Chang et al., 2003; Dulli et al., 2003).

Note to the Reader

Although this book specifically focuses on intimate partner violence in heterosexual relationships, understanding that different risks are associated for those in same-sex relationships is critical. Awareness of these issues and how they affect the care or lack of care received because of sexual orientation should be greater. No one should experience additional discrimination, barriers, ridicule, or oppression because of their sexual orientation, yet they often occur. Social workers must strengthen their knowledge and responses both individually and institutionally to better serve the lesbian, gay, bisexual, and transgendered (LGBT) population. These issues are further complicated by the intersection of race and sexual orientation, which includes multiple forms of oppression. Some basic facts to consider are as follows:

- Intimate partner violence does not occur more or less often in same-sex relationships.

- The perpetrator often uses threats to reveal the partner's sexual orientation to control or manipulate the survivor.

- Those becoming more secure in their sexual identity may interpret the violence as being a part of their sexual orientation, which is false. This false perception can create confusion when trying to obtain assistance.

- If the survivor has not revealed his or her sexual orientation, he or she could be further isolated from family and friends.

■ Service systems for people who experience domestic violence in same-sex relationships are not well developed. Shelter programs, domestic violence providers, and social service systems are often not prepared to address this dynamic, which increases the risk to the survivor.

Ignorance and discriminatory treatment can prevent someone from the LGBT community from obtaining services, calling the police, or talking to others about the abuse. This type of intolerance is unacceptable. As providers develop and reinvigorate services, consideration of how best to respond to the unique needs of the LGBT community must be a part of the discussion. All discrimination is wrong, and we all share responsibility to end oppression in all its forms.

Definitions and the Language of Domestic Violence

To understand the scope and prevalence of this problem, practitioners also have to understand the role that language and definitions play in responding to domestic violence. The definition of "domestic violence" is critical because, depending on the community, the language associated with domestic violence can be different. If a client defines "domestic violence" differently from the practitioner, then the disconnect is immediate and the chance of miscommunication increases. All of these terms are necessary to understand because although the differences are subtle, ensuring that people are communicating the same thoughts and ideas is important. Therefore, understanding the language often used in the field is important so that practitioners can talk across and within the profession and because "domestic violence" must be defined within the population to maximize effectiveness. Language is very important to build connections, limit misunderstandings, and enhance effectiveness. Many women do not want to go to a group labeled a "domestic violence" group, and some do not want to be labeled as a "victim." Some see a negative connotation in being referred to as "victims" or "battered women" and instead prefer "survivors" to highlight their resilience and ability to transcend the abuse. I use these words deliberately throughout the book to acknowledge those who are farther in healing and have survived the abuse (survivors) and those who have lost their lives due to abuse or continue to be victimized (victims). A great stigma still exists for women who seek services related to domestic violence. Therefore, although someone may be receiving domestic violence services, service providers must remember that the language of domestic violence can differ by population and using the terms "victim" or "battered woman" could turn people away from vital services.

Thus, it is increasingly important that social workers monitor their language. At the same time, someone may be experiencing domestic violence but not know that a term for or body of information about what they are facing exists. For example, one study examining attitudes and beliefs about domestic violence in the African American community found that the women viewed domestic violence as an issue predominantly affecting white women (Bent-Goodley, 2004a). They did not view verbal, mental, or psychological abuse or different forms of physical abuse, such as pushing, shoving, or slapping, as domestic violence. However, the women identified getting "beat up," for example, being punched, stabbed, shot, burned, and choked, as a high level of violence. These behaviors were considered to be domestic violence, more serious and warranting outside intervention. However, other forms of violence, such as emotional, verbal, or psychological abuse, were not viewed as domestic violence. Consequently, social workers must understand different populations' language related to domestic violence so that they can more effectively serve them. If practitioners force their definition of domestic violence on a population, it limits their ability to best serve that population. Practitioners have to take the time to understand how the community understands domestic violence so that they can best support them and help them. Often, the very language of domestic violence can bring up stigmas or negative perceptions. Therefore, ensuring that the language that practitioners use builds bridges as opposed to furthers a divide is that much more important.

The terminology used among professionals is also important to consider. "Domestic violence" has been used for a longer period of time and is more well known to those who may not follow the field. For others, the term "intimate partner violence" is more inclusive and provides an opportunity to better label emerging issues in the field. For still others, the term "gender-based violence" shows the connection between all forms of violence against women and connects violence experienced by women globally. These terms have important distinctions.

Terminology is also important from an interdisciplinary perspective because it determines how professionals respond to abuse. For example, most law enforcement officers do not arrest perpetrators for emotional, verbal, or psychological abuse. However, human service professionals view these dimensions as critical. Therefore, terminology is important in how professionals respond to domestic violence, and it guides how they interact with each other. It is important that social workers understand how terminology and language are used in the community and across professions to enhance communication and improve services to survivors, families, and communities.

Gender-based violence (GBV), as defined by Article 1 of the Declaration of the Elimination of Violence Against Women (UN General Assembly, 1993), is "physical, sexual or psychological harm or suffering to women, including threats of such acts, coercion or arbitrary deprivation of liberty, whether occurring in public or private life." GBV includes childhood sexual abuse, "prenatal sex selection in favor of boys, female infanticide, dowry deaths, honor killings, female genital mutilation, trafficking and forced prostitution, forced early marriage, sexual assault and intimate partner violence" (Bent-Goodley, 2009, p. 262). The term is often used by the global community and includes intimate partner violence, sexual violence, stalking, human trafficking, and other violent crimes committed against women because of their gender.

Wife abuse or *spousal abuse* is conceptualized as abuse that takes place between partners in a family system but excludes partners who are not married or are in same-sex relationships (Roberts, 2002). This term is dated and is less often used because it does not include people who are not married or are in same-sex relationships. However, it is important to acknowledge that it has been widely used in the literature.

Family violence is defined as the intentional intimidation or abuse of children, adults or elders by a family member, intimate partner or caretaker to gain power and control over the victim. Abuse has many forms including physical and sexual assault, emotional or psychological mistreatment, threats and intimidation, economic abuse and violation of individual rights. (Malley-Morrison & Hines, 2004, p. 5)

It has been used to describe violence within the family unit and includes intimate partner violence, sibling abuse, elder abuse, and child abuse and neglect. It is a broad term highlighting violence that takes place within the home.

Domestic violence is defined as "a pattern of assaultive and coercive behaviors including physical, sexual, and psychological attacks, as well as economic coercion that adults or adolescents use against their intimate partners" (Schechter & Ganley, 1995, p. 10). This definition highlights the patterns of behavior rooted in the concept of using power to control another person physically, sexually, economically, and psychologically.

Intimate partner violence has been defined as "physical, sexual, or psychological harm by a current or former intimate partner or spouse. This type of violence can occur among heterosexual or same-sex couples" (National Institute of Justice, 2010). Intimate partner violence speaks to the idea that violence can take place between partners regardless of where they live. I use "domestic violence" and "intimate partner violence" interchangeably throughout the book.

Cultural Context

The cultural context of domestic violence is vital to being able to understand and appreciate how domestic violence uniquely affects different populations. Cultural context includes historical experiences of oppression; contemporary realities of discrimination; customs, traditions, and practices that can serve as barriers and strengths in the population; and intergenerational exchanges about culture that inform the knowledge, thinking, experiences, and perceived realities of communities of color. If social workers are to address domestic violence effectively across diverse populations, they must understand cultural context to connect and build trust with these communities (Bent-Goodley, 2004b, 2005; Burman, Smailes, & Chantler, 2004; Campbell et al., 2008). Culture has often been separated from how domestic violence is defined and understood, which is a major error because cultural context informs how a group understands and experiences domestic violence.

One must also understand how domestic violence affects diverse communities differently. African American and Native American women are at the highest risk for victimization compared with other groups of women. African American women experience victimization at a rate 35 percent higher than white women and 22 percent higher than other women of color (Rennison, 2003). Domestic violence rates among African Americans are essentially the same as rates among white women when controlling for income, with those ages 20 to 24 at the greatest risk of experiencing abuse (Rennison, 2003). Latinas also experience their highest risk of violence at ages 20 to 24. Nearly 13 percent of Asian and Pacific Islander women experience abuse. The lack of awareness of differential factors and impacts within communities of color can impede finding effective and lasting solutions. In fact, this book does not have a chapter on culture because I have integrated cultural context throughout the book, as it should be in social work practice and research. Domestic violence is not the same for every person. Although the physical injuries may be similar in nature, how women receive assistance, access support, and are perceived differs on the basis of their race or ethnicity. To serve diverse communities most effectively, it is critical that social workers understand their cultural experience and dynamics. A lack of knowledge or limited understanding of the cultural context can diminish the effectiveness of the services provided, which is counter to what practitioners are trying to do. If practitioners do not understand the group that they are working with, they will be less likely to serve them effectively. Therefore, understanding the cultural context should never be optional. It must be integrated into service provision as part of sound ethical practice so that practitioners can best serve diverse populations and meet their needs. Being culturally competent is about more than hiring direct service staff or paraprofessionals to work with clients, it is about making a commitment to ensuring that diversity ideologically and directly influences decision making and leadership across all levels of an institution. People from the community should be equal partners and participate proportionally as part of the institution's leadership, including the board of directors. Being culturally proficient is not a vague concept. Specific issues affect how diverse communities experience intimate partner violence, and important cultural contexts are associated with help-seeking behaviors, coping strategies, cultural values, fear of police, skepticism of the court system, the historical context, the intersectionality of oppression, and institutional racism and discrimination (Bent-Goodley, 2007; Sokoloff, 2005; C. M. West, 2003, 2005; T. C. West, 1999).

Delayed Help-Seeking Behaviors

Although women may endure violence in a relationship because they view it as a personal matter, do not know it is wrong, or are living in fear, they may be compelled to report domestic violence when they feel their life is seriously threatened or if they feel that they could harm their partner as a result of the violence. As such, help seeking is often delayed and usually occurs when the violence could have serious physical consequences or is potentially lethal, particularly for women of color. Women of color often first reach out to family and friends to deal with violence in the home (Bent-Goodley, 2001; Fontes & McCloskey, 2011; Vidales, 2010; T. C. West, 1999). Their first attempt to resolve the violence is usually in the informal system. If they are met with indifference or resistance, they could be pushed further away from resolving the problem. Simultaneously, women may need formal supports to assist them but may not feel comfortable exposing the violence because of feelings of shame or embarrassment for themselves and their community. Delayed help seeking can place women at grave risk for further and more intense violence and victimization.

Coping Strategies

Coping strategies have also been found to be different among women. Women of color are more likely to use religious or spiritual coping factors than are white women in similar situations (Bent-Goodley & Fowler, 2006; Hassouneh-Phillips, 2003; Watlington & Murphy, 2006). Following friends and family members, African American women turn to their religious institutions before formal provider systems (Bent-Goodley, 2007; Ellison & Anderson, 2001; Ellison, Trinitapoli, Anderson, & Johnson, 2007; T. C. West, 1999). Some women seek spiritual guidance and support through prayer and meditation. However, some women seek the support of their religious community, including sacred scripture and ministry groups. Recognizing and validating this coping mechanism is key to assisting women of faith to create and identify safe solutions to address domestic violence. Faith also speaks to the hope and resilience of many women of faith. Harnessing this important coping mechanism is critical from the stance of providing effective services, particularly for women of color who are more likely to use these coping mechanisms.

Cultural Values

The importance of family and community is a traditional cultural value that has sustained people of color (Bent-Goodley, 2009; Carlton-LaNey, 2001; Hill, 1997; Kasturirangan, Krishnan, & Riger, 2004; Martin & Martin, 2002). Women of color often feel a particular responsibility to sustain the family and make necessary self-sacrifices not just for the family, but also to not bring shame to the community, as divulging domestic violence may be perceived as a source of collective shame (Richie, 1996). They are also charged with keeping the family together and advancing the community. This value of communalism, often cited as a strength, can make it difficult for women of color to share what they are experiencing despite safety and health risks associated with the silence. Formal systems, particularly law enforcement and court systems, are not viewed as being designed to protect them. As a result, many women of color feel unprotected and as though they should take their safety into their own hands. Issues of race may be viewed as more important than issues of gender, resulting in a deprioritization of gender (Potter, 2008). Therefore, family and community, roles, and expectations are key constructs to understand for this population.

Fear of Police

The police are often not viewed as a source of support among people of color (Bent-Goodley, 2004a; Bent-Goodley & Williams, 2005; Richie, 1996). Some women fear that their partner will be harmed or treated unfairly if the police are contacted. In addition, they may be uncomfortable with the way in which the police interact not only with the perpetrator, but also with the survivor. Some women have found that the police are often disrespectful, appear uninterested, and despite mandatory arrest laws, do not arrest the batterer. Police response has also been highlighted as poor, with police arriving too late after the incident, putting the woman at greater risk, particularly in high-poverty communities. These issues are important because in many communities the police provide the first point of access to stopping the violence. Thus, to respond to domestic violence in communities of color, the poor relationship with law enforcement must be addressed.

Skepticism of the Court System

Women of color are more likely than white women to be skeptical of the court system's interest in and willingness to protect them (Bent-Goodley & Williams, 2005). Courts are often associated with disproportionate incarceration of people of color. For these reasons, many women do not view the court system as a place to get help. Disproportionate criminal justice responses and disproportionate minority contact converge to create a sense of mistrust between those affiliated with the criminal justice system and people of color who need help. Consequently, the criminal justice system is not seen as an ally but is instead viewed as more harmful than helpful.

Immigration and Intimate Partner Violence

Immigration status can be used by the perpetrator to control the survivor through manipulation of immigration laws, language barriers, social isolation, lack of financial resources, and inability to access public supports (Dutton, Orloff, & Hass, 2000; Kasturirangan et al., 2004). The complexity of the situation results in many survivors remaining hidden and unidentified (Engstrom & Okamura, 2007). Coupled with systems located outside of the community and the lack of cultural and linguistic competence, women of color often have great difficulty negotiating these issues at the institutional level (Ely, 2004; Vidales, 2010). However, the Violence Against Women Act as updated in 2000 with the Battered Immigrant Women Protection Act (P.L. 106-386) has offered some sanctuary for immigrant women experiencing domestic violence. Once the woman is determined to have experienced domestic violence, her immigration status can be adjusted under the law to keep her safe and not penalize her for experiencing the abuse (Bhuyan, 2008). Several provisions for immigrant women include filing a self-petition without the help or knowledge of the perpetrator, requesting a "cancellation of removal" to avoid deportation, and requesting a waiver. These provisions are critical to understand so that women can be better informed of the options available to them. However, immigration status continues to pose a major concern in communities of color, particularly if the person is undocumented.

Historical and Contemporary Context

Historical context has been identified as being critical to understanding how people of color have experienced domestic violence (Bent-Goodley, 2004a, 2005; Bent-Goodley & Williams, 2005; Grossman & Lundy, 2007; Martin & Martin, 2002; T. C. West, 1999). The historical experience of enslavement, Jim Crow laws, and ongoing intolerance and discrimination has affected the nature of black male–female relationships in terms of communication patterns, gender expectations, and gender socialization (Bent-Goodley, 2001; Potter, 2008). Although challenging enough by themselves, the issues are even more complex when considered in terms of how they intersect (Bent-Goodley, 2005; Sokoloff, 2005). Native American scholars have identified how historical trauma and the disenfranchisement of Native people have affected domestic violence in the Native American community and specifically how that trauma is linked to the inequity and discrimination experienced by the Native American population (Engstrom & Okamura, 2007; Hart & Lowther, 2008; Willmon-Haque & BigFoot, 2008). The Latino community has identified several critical institutional and systemic barriers to obtaining supports, including institutional racism and discrimination as they relate to immigration status, the lack of cultural and linguistic services, and limited providers who understand cultural issues specific to diverse Latino experiences, such as the challenge of acculturation and intergenerational transmission of culture (Ingram, 2007; Klevens, 2007; Sorenson, 2006). The Asian American community has also struggled with a system that does little to recognize its needs and unique struggles, particularly as related to cultural dynamics that may support domestic violence in their country of origin and the challenges of being isolated in this country physically while practicing the traditions and customs of their country of origin (Cheung, Leung, & Tsui, 2009; Yick, 2007; Yick & Oomen-Early, 2008; Yoshioka, Gilbert, El-Bassel, & Baig-Amin, 2003). These cultural experiences must be acknowledged if social work is to best serve and support these diverse populations. Comprehensive services rooted in understanding the cultural context and being able to apply that knowledge using a biopsychosocial–spiritual framework are necessary to respond to these issues.

In 2001, the social work profession adopted standards for cultural competence in social work practice that include 10 essential components:

1. Social workers should be able to meet the needs of a diverse client base, which is viewed as part of ethical practice.

2. Practitioners must possess self-awareness and appreciate diversity.

3. Social workers should have an understanding of the history, traditions, and customs of the client population they serve.

4. Social workers should possess the skills needed to engage and work with diverse populations.

5. Social workers should be aware of services and service availability issues for diverse populations.

6. Social workers should be aware of how policies and practices affect diverse client populations and have a commitment to advocacy for and empowerment of those populations.

7. The social work workforce should include diversity at all levels of practice and administration.

8. Social workers should engage in continuing education that will strengthen their practice throughout their professional career with a focus on meeting the needs of diverse populations.

9. Social workers must be able to meet the needs of various linguistic populations, including obtaining interpreter services to support practice.

10. Social workers should be able to articulate the needs and experiences of cross-cultural groups to other professionals, in the community, and among colleagues (NASW, 2001).

The profession has used these standards to require a commitment to integrate cultural competence into practice and recognize the importance of this issue for all practitioners. Cultural competence requires that practitioners create solutions and recognize the person from a holistic stance. The cultural issues identified earlier provide a framework for understanding how to consider issues related to responding to domestic violence among communities of color. Table 1-1 illustrates the importance of using a mind–body–social–spiritual framework to working with people of color as related to domestic violence.

Table 1-1: Mind–Body–Social–Spiritual Domestic Violence Framework

Mind	Body	Social	Spiritual
• Cognitive well-being • Thought processes • Perception of options • Cultural awareness • Communication patterns • Identity • Neurocognitive functioning	• Location of resources • Health disparities • Physical impact of abuse • Access to care • Quality of care	• Institutional barriers • Cultural traditions • Culturally competent practices • Value system • Traditions • Customs • Language • Social determinants • Socioeconomic status • Education • Help-seeking • Myths and stereotypes • Family and community expectations • Impact of racism and discrimination • Immigration status	• Coping • Resilience • Hope • Religious practices • Prayer • Informal support systems

Reflecting Pool

In this chapter, I explored the terminology used in the area of domestic violence. I also examined the scope and prevalence of the problem. Recognizing the importance of being able to contextualize these terms, I sought to give you an understanding of how many women experience and struggle with this issue, so that you can contextualize what you will learn in the rest of the book. In this part of the Reflecting Pool, think about your terminology and your perception of domestic violence. I challenge you to consider where your definition comes from. Think about and consider how your definition shapes your thinking, action, and perceptions of people who experience and perpetrate abuse. As I challenge you in the Reflecting Pool, I also hope to provide you with insight into how I have challenged myself in my own evolution.

My Reflection

As a newly graduated social worker, I knew that one day I would be confronted with a client experiencing domestic violence. What I did not understand was the complexity of the issue. I certainly did not understand the prevalence, scope, and magnitude of domestic violence, and so as a new practitioner I did not expect to find domestic violence in so many of my cases. Being able to challenge myself to understand how pervasive this issue was gave me a better appreciation of why I needed to develop my knowledge and skills in this area. Understanding the sheer magnitude of the problem made me realize that to best serve children and families, I had to better equip myself to address domestic violence. I began to search for opportunities to learn more, going above and beyond continuing education requirements to a fuller understanding of the complexity of intimate partner violence and how it differentially affects the populations I served. I attended conferences and trainings, read books, and contacted experts and providers to ensure that I fully understood the issue and how I could best respond as a practitioner.

Your Reflection

Here are some questions I want you to explore before you move on to the next chapter. This is the place for you to safely examine your thinking about the scope of the problem and what you have learned. In addition, consider the cultural implications of the work you do and how domestic violence crosses many different population groups.

- What do you think about the statistics and what they tell us about the prevalence of domestic violence?

- How do you think domestic violence may reveal itself among your clients?

- How do you perceive domestic violence?

- What language or terms do you use to identify domestic violence?

- Explore what you believe intimate partner violence looks like. Who do you believe are the victims?

- What are your perceptions of domestic violence across diverse populations?

- How would you go about strengthening your knowledge and skills to practice in this area or include a focus on this issue in your practice?

- What role do you believe income plays with regard to domestic violence?

Notes:

_____

_____

_____

_____

_____

_____

_____

_____

_____

_____

References

Adams, D. (2007). *Why do they kill: Men who murder their intimate partners.* Nashville, TN: Vanderbilt University Press.

Administration on Aging. (2007). *Older Americans Act.* Retrieved from http://www.aoa.gov/aoaroot/aoa_programs/oaa/oaa_full.asp

Baker, C., Cook, S., & Norris, F. (2003). Domestic violence and housing problems: A contextual analysis of women's help-seeking, received informal support and formal system response. *Violence Against Women, 9,* 754–783.

Baladerian, N. J. (2009). Domestic violence and individuals with disabilities: Reflections on research and practice. *Journal of Aggression, Maltreatment & Trauma, 18,* 153–161.

Battered Immigrant Women Protection Act of 2000, P.L. 106-386, Div. B. Title V, 114 Stat. 1518.

Beaulaurier, R., Seff, L., Newman, F., & Dunlop, B. (2007). External barriers to help seeking for older women who experience intimate partner violence. *Journal of Family Violence, 22,* 747–755.

Bent-Goodley, T. B. (2001). Eradicating domestic violence in the African American community: A literature review and action agenda. *Trauma, Violence, and Abuse, 2,* 316–330.

Bent-Goodley, T. B. (2004a). Perceptions of domestic violence: A dialogue with African American women. *Health & Social Work, 29,* 307–316.

Bent-Goodley, T. B. (2004b). Policy implications of domestic violence for people of color. In K. E. Davis & T. B. Bent-Goodley (Eds.), *The color of social policy* (pp. 65–80). Alexandria, VA: Council on Social Work Education.

Bent-Goodley, T. B. (2005). Culture and domestic violence: Transforming knowledge development. *Journal of Interpersonal Violence, 20,* 195–203.

Bent-Goodley, T. B. (2007). Health disparities and violence against women: Why and how cultural and societal influences matter. *Trauma, Violence & Abuse, 8,* 90–104.

Bent-Goodley, T. B. (2009). A black experience–based approach to gender-based violence. *Social Work, 54,* 262–269.

Bent-Goodley, T. B., & Fowler, D. N. (2006). Spiritual and religious abuse: Expanding what is known about domestic violence. *Affilia: Journal of Women and Social Work, 21,* 282–295.

Bent-Goodley, T. B., & Williams, O. J. (2005). *Community insights on domestic violence among African Americans: Conversations about domestic violence and other issues affecting their community, Seattle, Washington.* St. Paul, MN: Institute on Domestic Violence in the African American Community.

Bhuyan, R. (2008). The production of the "battered immigrant" in public policy and domestic violence advocacy. *Journal of Interpersonal Violence, 23,* 153–170.

Block, C. (2003, November). How can practitioners help an abused women lower her risk of death? *NIJ Journal, 250,* 5–7.

Burman, E., Smailes, S., & Chantler, K. (2004). "Culture" as a barrier to service provision and delivery: Domestic violence services for minoritized women. *Critical Social Policy, 24,* 332–357.

Campbell, J., Campbell, D., Gary, F., Nedd, D., Price-Lea, P., Sharps, P., & Smith, C. (2008). African American women's responses to intimate partner violence: An examination of cultural context. *Journal of Aggression, Maltreatment & Trauma, 16,* 277–295.

Campbell, J., Glass, N., Sharps, P., Laughon, K., & Bloom, T. (2007). Intimate partner violence. *Trauma, Violence & Abuse, 8,* 246–269.

Campbell, J. C., Webster, D., Koziol-McLain, J., Block, C., Campbell, D., Curry, M. A., & Laughon, K. (2003). Risk factors for femicide in abusive relationships: Results from a multi-site case control study. *American Journal of Public Health, 93,* 1089–1097.

Carlton-LaNey, I. B. (Ed.). (2001). *African American leadership: An empowerment tradition in social welfare history.* Washington, DC: NASW Press.

Catalano, S. (2007). *Intimate partner violence in the United States.* Washington, DC: Bureau of Justice Statistics.

Centers for Disease Control and Prevention. (2008). Adverse health conditions and health risk behaviors associated with intimate partner violence. *Morbidity and Mortality Weekly Report, 57,* 113–117.

Chang, J. C., Martin, S. L., Moracco, K. E., Dulli, L., Scandlin, D., Loucks-Sorrel, M. B., & Bou-Saada, I. (2003). Helping women with disabilities and domestic violence: Strategies, limitations, and challenges of domestic violence programs and services. *Journal of Women's Health, 12,* 699–708.

Chesler, P. (2009). Are honor killings simply domestic violence? *Middle East Quarterly, 16,* 61–69.

Cheung, M., Leung, P., & Tsui, V. (2009). Asian male domestic violence victims: Services exclusive for men. *Journal of Family Violence, 24,* 447–462.

Commonwealth Fund. (1999). *Health concerns across a woman's lifespan: 1998 survey of women's health.* New York: Author.

Dulli, L., Scandlin, D., Turner, T., Starsoneck, L., Dorian, P., & Bou-Saada, I. (2003). Helping women with disabilities and domestic violence: Strategies, limitation, and challenges of domestic violence programs and services. *Journal of Women's Health, 12,* 699–708.

Durose, M., Harlow, C., Langan, P., Motivans, M., Rantala, R., & Smith, E. (2005). *Family violence statistics: Including statistics on strangers and acquaintances* (NCJ 207846). Washington, DC: Bureau of Justice Statistics.

Dutton, M., Orloff, L., & Hass, G. A. (2000). Characteristics of help-seeking behaviors, resources, and services needs of battered immigrant Latinas: Legal and policy implications. *Georgetown Journal on Poverty Law and Policy, 7,* 245–305.

Ellison, C. G., & Anderson, K. L. (2001). Religious involvement and domestic violence among U.S. couples. *Journal for the Scientific Study of Religion, 40,* 269–286.

Ellison, C. G., Trinitapoli, J. A., Anderson, K. L., & Johnson, B. R. (2007). Race/ethnicity, religious involvement, and domestic violence. *Violence Against Women, 13,* 1094–1112.

Ely, G. (2004). Domestic violence and immigrant communities in the United States: A review of women's unique needs and recommendations for social work practice and research. *Stress, Trauma & Crisis: An International Journal, 7,* 223–241.

Engstrom, D., & Okamura, A. (2007). A nation of immigrants: A call for a specialization in immigrant well-being. *Journal of Ethnic and Cultural Diversity in Social Work, 16,* 103–111.

Fontes, L., & McCloskey, K. (2011). Cultural issues in violence against women. In C. M. Renzetti, J. L. Edleson, & R. K. Bergen (Eds.), *Sourcebook on violence against women* (2nd ed., pp. 151–168.) Thousand Oaks, CA: Sage Publications.

Garcia-Moreno, C., Jansen, H., Ellsberg, M., Heise, L., & Watts, C. (2005). *WHO multi-country study on women's health and domestic violence against women: Initial results on prevalence health outcomes and women's health and domestic violence.* Geneva, Switzerland: World Health Organization.

Goodwin, S., Chandler, D., & Meisel, J. (2003). *Violence against women: The role of welfare reform.* Washington, DC: National Institute of Justice.

Grossman, S. F., & Lundy, M. (2003). Use of domestic violence services across race and ethnicity by women aged 55 and older. *Violence Against Women, 9,* 1442–1452.

Grossman, S. F., & Lundy, M. (2007). Domestic violence across race and ethnicity: Implications for social work practice and policy. *Violence Against Women, 13,* 1029–1052.

Hart, R. A., & Lowther, M. A. (2008). Honoring sovereignty: Aiding tribal efforts to protect Native American women from domestic violence. *California Law Review, 96,* 185–233.

Hassouneh-Phillips, D. (2003). Strength and vulnerability: Spirituality in abused American Muslim women's lives. *Issues in Mental Health Nursing, 24,* 681–694.

Hill, R. B. (1997). *The strengths of African American families: Twenty-five years later.* Washington, DC: R & B.

Ingram, E. M. (2007). A comparison of help seeking between Latino and non-Latino victims of intimate partner violence. *Violence Against Women, 13,* 159–171.

Kasturirangan, A., Krishnan, S., & Riger, S. (2004). The impact of culture and minority status on women's experience of domestic violence. *Trauma, Violence & Abuse, 5,* 318–332.

Kilbane, T., & Spira, M. (2010). Domestic violence or elder abuse? Why it matters for older women. *Families in Society, 91,* 165–170.

Klevens, J. (2007). An overview of intimate partner violence among Latinos. *Violence Against Women, 13,* 111–122.

Leisey, M., Kupstas, P. K., & Cooper, A. (2009). Domestic violence in the second half of life. *Journal of Elder Abuse & Neglect, 21,* 141–155.

Levendosky, A., Bogat, G., Theran, S., Trotter, J., von Eye, A., & Davidson, W. (2004). The social networks of women experiencing domestic violence. *American Journal of Community Psychology, 34,* 95–109.

Lightfoot, E., & Williams, O. (2009). The intersection of disability, diversity, and domestic violence: Results of national focus groups. *Journal of Aggression, Maltreatment & Trauma, 18,* 133–152.

Logan, T., Shannon, L., Walker, R., & Faragher, T. (2006). Protective orders: Questions and conundrums. *Trauma, Violence & Abuse, 7,* 175–205.

Lundy, M., & Grossman, S. F. (2004). Elder abuse: Spouse/intimate partner abuse and family violence among elders. *Journal of Elder Abuse & Neglect, 16,* 85–102.

Lundy, M., & Grossman, S. (2009). Domestic violence service users: A comparison of older and younger women victims. *Journal of Family Violence, 24,* 297–309.

Malley-Morrison, K., & Hines, D. (2004). *Family violence in a cultural perspective: Defining, understanding, and combating abuse.* Thousand Oaks, CA: Sage Publications.

Martin, E. P., & Martin, J. M. (2002). *Spirituality and the black helping tradition in social work.* Washington, DC: NASW Press.

Mays, J. (2006). Feminist disability theory: Domestic violence against women with a disability. *Disability & Society, 21,* 147–158.

National Association of Social Workers. (2001). *NASW standards for cultural competence in social work practice.* Washington, DC: Author.

National Center for Injury Prevention and Control. (2003). *Costs of intimate partner violence against women in the United States.* Atlanta: Centers for Disease Control and Prevention.

National Institute of Justice. (2010). *Intimate partner violence.* Retrieved from http://www.ojp.usdoj.gov/nij/topics/crime/intimate-partner-violence/

National Network to End Domestic Violence. (2009). *Domestic violence counts 2009: A 24-hour census of domestic violence shelters and services.* Washington, DC: Author.

Nixon, J. (2009). Domestic violence and women with disabilities: Locating the issue on the periphery of social movements. *Disability & Society, 24,* 77–89.

Otto, J., & Quinn, K. (2007, May). *Barriers to and promising practices for collaboration between adult protective services and domestic violence programs.* Washington, DC: National Center on Elder Abuse.

Potter, H. (2008). *Battle cries: Black women and intimate partner abuse.* New York: New York University Press.

Rand, M. R., & Saltzman, L. E. (2003). The nature and extent of recurring intimate partner violence against women in the United States. *Journal of Comparative Family Studies, 34,* 137–149.

Rennison, C. M. (2003). *Intimate partner violence, 1993–2001* (NCJ 197838). Washington, DC: Bureau of Justice Statistics.

Rennison, C. M., & Welchans, S. (2002). Bureau of Justice Statistics special report: Intimate partner violence. BJS Statisticians. Retrieved from http://www.ojp.usdoj.gov/bjs/pub/pdf/ipv.pdf

Richie, B. E. (1996). *Compelled to crime: The gender entrapment of battered black women.* New York: Routledge.

Roberts, A. R. (2002). *Handbook of domestic violence intervention strategies: Policies, programs and legal remedies.* New York: Oxford University Press.

Schechter, S., & Ganley, A. L. (1995). *A national curriculum for family preservation practitioners.* San Francisco: Family Violence Prevention Fund.

Slayter, E. (2009). Intimate partner violence against women with disabilities: Implications for disability service system case management practice. *Journal of Aggression, Maltreatment and Trauma, 18,* 182–199.

Smith, E., & Farole, D. (2009). *Profile of intimate partner violence cases in large urban counties* (NCJ 228193). Washington, DC: Bureau of Justice Statistics.

Sokoloff, N. J. (Ed.). (2005). *Domestic violence at the margins: Readings on race, class, gender, and culture.* New Brunswick, NJ: Rutgers University Press.

Sorenson, S. B. (2006). Taking guns from batterers: Public support and policy implications. *Evaluation Review, 30,* 361–373.

Straka, S. M., & Montminy, L. (2006). Responding to the needs of older women experiencing domestic violence. *Violence Against Women, 12,* 251–267.

Tjaden, P., & Thoennes, N. (2000). *Extent, nature, and consequences of violence against women: Findings from the National Violence Against Women Survey* (NCJ 181867). Washington, DC: Bureau of Justice Statistics.

Trotter, J., & Allen, N. (2009). The good, the bad, and the ugly: Domestic violence survivors' experiences with their informal social networks. *American Journal of Community Psychology, 43,* 221–231.

United Nations Development Fund for Women. (2003). *Not a minute more: Ending violence against women.* New York: Author.

UN General Assembly. (1993). *Declaration on the elimination of violence against women* (A/RES/48/104). Retrieved from http://www.unhcr.org/ref-world/docid/3b00f25d2c.html

U.S. Conference of Mayors. (2003, December). *Sodexho hunger and homeless-ness survey.* Washington, DC: Author.

U.S. Department of Justice. (2009, September). *Homicide trends in the United States.* Retrieved from http://bjs.ojp.usdoj.gov/content/pub/pdf/htius.pdf

Vidales, G. (2010). Arrested justice: The multifaceted plight of immigrant Latinas who faced domestic violence. *Journal of Family Violence, 25,* 533–544.

Violence Policy Center. (2004, September). *When men murder women: An analysis of 2002 homicide data—Females murdered by males in single victim/single offender incidents.* Washington, DC: Author.

Watlington, C. G., & Murphy, C. M. (2006). The roles of religion and spiri-tuality among African American survivors of domestic violence. *Journal of Clinical Psychology, 62,* 837–857.

West, C. M. (Ed.). (2003). *Violence in the lives of black women: Battered, black and blue.* New York: Routledge.

West, C. M. (2005). Domestic violence in ethnically and racially diverse families: The "political gag order" has been lifted. In N. Sokoloff & C. Pratt (Eds.), *Domestic violence at the margins: Readings on race, class, gender and culture* (pp. 157–173). New Brunswick, NJ: Rutgers University Press.

West, T. C. (1999). *Wounds of the spirit: Black women, violence, and resistance ethics.* New York: New York University Press.

Wilke, D., & Vinton, L. (2005). The nature and impact of domestic violence across age cohorts. *Affilia: Journal of Women and Social Work, 20,* 316–328.

Williams, S., & Mickelson, K. (2004). The nexus of domestic violence and poverty. *Violence Against Women, 10,* 283–293.

Willmon-Haque, S., & BigFoot, S. D. (2008). Violence and the effects of trauma on American Indian and Alaska Native populations. *Journal of Emotional Abuse, 8,* 51–66.

Yick, A. G. (2007). Role of culture and context: Ethical issues in research with Asian Americans and immigrants in intimate violence. *Journal of Family Violence, 22,* 277–285.

Yick, A. G., & Oomen-Early, J. (2008). A 16-year examination of domestic violence among Asians and Asian Americans in the empirical knowledge base: A content analysis. *Journal of Interpersonal Violence, 23,* 1075–1094.

Yoshioka, M. R., Gilbert, L., El-Bassel, N., & Baig-Amin, M. (2003). Social support and disclosure of abuse: Comparing South Asian, African American, and Hispanic battered women. *Journal of Family Violence, 18,* 171–180.

Select Resources

- *An Abuse, Race, and Domestic Violence Aid and Resource Collection:* http://www.aardvarc.org/dv/gay.shtml

- *Alianza: National Latino Alliance for the Elimination of Domestic Violence:* http://www.dvalianza.org/

- *Asian and Pacific Islander Institute on Domestic Violence:* http://www.apiahf.org/index.php/programs/domestic-violence.html

- *Centers for Disease Control and Prevention:* http://www.cdc.gov/ViolencePrevention/intimatepartnerviolence/index.html

- *Family Violence Prevention Fund:* http://endabuse.org/

- *Institute on Domestic Violence in the African American Community:* http://www.idvaac.org/

- *National Center for Victims of Crime:* http://www.ncvc.org/ncvc/main.aspx?dbName=DocumentViewer&DocumentID=32347

- *National Resource Center on Domestic Violence:* http://www.nrcdv.org/

- *Tribal Court Clearinghouse:* http://www.tribal-institute.org/lists/domestic.htm

- *Women of Color Network:* http://womenofcolornetwork.org/

Two

Causes of Intimate Partner Violence

Inevitably, someone asks me, "What causes domestic violence"? In this chapter, I focus on helping you understand the causes of domestic violence and the different theories that have been used to explain it. Many myths regarding what causes domestic violence exist, and I examine some of these myths and offer some thoughts about each. Theory is used as a way to explain behavior and provides an opportunity to understand and categorize the different behaviors that social workers see in practice. Theories do not provide a definite scenario, meaning they do not suggest these are the only reasons for domestic violence or that every situation can be explained by one theory. Theory is used as a guide to explore what could be happening in a given situation. It provides an opportunity to anchor individual experiences in a collective context. Theory provides a context for what you may find in the field and should help you understand what you see in your daily practice. You will also find that an integrated set of theories, as opposed to one single theory used to explain varied experiences, often best guides your practice. Once you determine the theory or set of theories you are working with, then you can develop more targeted approaches and interventions to best assist the client.

Psychological Theories

Psychological theories focus on individual characteristics that cause the perpetration of and experiences related to intimate partner violence. These theories are based on the idea of psychopathology or personality disorders that affect an individual's behavior. The idea that psychological issues cause violent outbursts, the inability to control one's behavior, and low self-esteem converge into psychological theories. Psychological issues include borderline personality disorder, bipolar disorder, antisocial personality disorder, and schizophrenia.

"Violent husbands evidence more psychological distress, more tendencies to personality disorders, more attachment/dependency problems, more anger/hostility, and more alcohol problems than nonviolent men" (Holtzworth-Munroe, Bates, Smutzler, & Sandin, 1997, p. 94).

Personality disorders account for most of the psychological issues among perpetrators, with many perpetrators evidencing poor impulse control, outbursts, poor self-esteem, and high levels of jealousy (Hart, Dutton, & Newlove, 1993). Yet only 10 percent of cases of perpetrators fit this profile.

Battered women's syndrome has also been discussed from a psychological perspective. It is regarded as a subcategory of posttraumatic stress disorder whereby the survivor reexperiences the violence when it is not occurring, experiences hypervigilance, and has issues with self-image and self-esteem (Walker, 2006). The woman may also experience problems with intimacy and challenges in maintaining personal relationships.

Social Learning Theory

Social learning theory postulates that people emulate behaviors they have seen and learned in their environment, particularly if the behavior has no negative consequences. These influences are not limited to family systems but also include the larger society, such as media outlets, community issues, and other ecological considerations. Those people who subscribe to social learning theory believe that intimate partner violence is a learned behavior. Social learning theory is often connected to intergenerational violence, which means that the violence that perpetrators use and the violence survivors experience are a result of witnessing violence in their home as children (Wareham, Boots, & Chavez, 2009). Intergenerational patterns then speak to violence experienced as a cycle across generations of a family. Certainly, situations exist in which one can argue the idea that domestic violence is learned and passed down from generation to generation (Corvo, Dutton, & Wan-Yi, 2008; Holtzworth-Munroe et al., 1997; Ornduff, Kelsey, & O'Leary, 2001; Pears & Capaldi, 2001). It does represent a risk factor for either experiencing or perpetrating abuse later in life and is something that social workers have to know and understand as practitioners working with families. However, witnessing domestic violence as a child does not conclusively mean the child will experience or perpetrate it as an adult (Holt, Buckley, & Whelan, 2008). An additional key factor of social learning theory is the idea of positive and negative reinforcement. If someone experiences abuse with a negative consequence or if someone perpetrates abuse without a negative consequence, then the behavior has been reinforced. The idea is that being exposed to something is in and of itself not reason for someone to reproduce the behavior. However, positive or negative reinforcement of the behavior can either reinforce or deter the method used. If someone is abusive to a partner and that behavior carries no consequence, then society has positively reinforced the behavior because of the lack of a negative consequence. Social learning theory encourages practitioners to consider other influences outside of the relationship and how they reinforce perceptions of intimate partner violence.

Resource Theory

Resource theory also provides an explanation for intimate partner violence. The notion behind resource theory is that those who hold the most resources have more power and control in a relationship. The idea is that if, in a relationship, both partners have equal status and equal resources, then there will be less likelihood of violence in the relationship. However, if the balance of resources within the relationship is unequal, then the risk for violence will increase. Using this theory, one of the causes of violence is that women are not able to walk away from a violent situation because of their dependency on the relationship. If a person lacks power and control in the relationship because he or she lacks economic or social resources and the other person has more power because he or she possesses these resources, then the partner with more resources could resort to using violence because the other person has no power in the relationship and lacks the necessary resources to get out of the situation. More important, social workers must recognize that the resource is not always economic.

For example, for many African American women, the resource is not the economic situation but the social context (Potter, 2008). The woman could make a higher income or be receiving public assistance. However, because of the perception that the number of marriageable African American men is limited (Bent-Goodley, 2009), the woman may feel more inclined to stay in the relationship because she feels she has a limited pool of men from which to select. The consequence is that she may consider and stay in a relationship because of the limited resource—the perceived limited number of marriageable men in her community—which could place her at risk. Immigration status could also be aligned with resource theory, in that immigration status can be viewed as a resource, making one partner more powerful in the relationship and the other less powerful. Thus, resource theory is important to consider beyond economic issues and inclusive of other forms of resources.

Ecological Theory

Ecological theory encourages the practitioner to examine the environmental influences. Being able to identify environmental influences and how they affect decision making is very important as it relates to intimate partner violence. Those who ascribe to this theory believe that people do not live alone in the world and no one is an island. Consequently, people are a part of a larger community and part of a broader society with different levels of environmental influences. A basic idea behind the ecological approach is that to understand why intimate partner violence occurs, one has to understand the environment in which people live. The idea is that violence in relationships is a result of having different environmental influences. For example, looking at the immediate family system, one might have seen or witnessed violence within an intimate relationship. When that violence is coupled with a community that itself might be experiencing high levels of violence, the risk increases. Then, one has to consider the higher level of societal violence, violence that is often used as a remedy for or a mechanism of resolving problems. When levels of violence across ecological influences are examined, one sees that the environment has an impact on relationships and becomes an important construct. The ecological approach makes one think about the idea that people are influenced by and have different experiences because of the environment in which they live and that someone who lives in a community plagued with poverty and violence might have a greater risk for experiencing intimate partner violence because of the nature of the community in which he or she lives. The environment affects how people resolve issues and problems not just in their community but also in their families. The influence of the environment becomes critically important. The influence of schools; faith communities; civic, fraternity, and sorority organizations; and grassroots organizations could ease or buffer negative ecological factors and how they affect intimate partner violence. The ecological approach challenges one to think beyond the individual and acknowledge that intimate partner violence is not a private problem and is not limited to one home, one family, one community, or one group of people. The theory reinforces that intimate partner violence goes beyond the individual and the family and speaks to the larger environmental and ecological constructs that affect relationships.

Social Stress Theory

Social stress theory asserts that stressors have an impact on violence experienced or perpetrated in relationships. The idea behind this theory is not just that stress affects behavior, but that multiple stressors affect people and their decision making. Those who believe in this notion of social stress would argue that stress is experienced physiologically, psychologically, emotionally, and socially and that physiological changes can increase tension and anxiety. Financial stressors can create feelings of desperation to obtain resources, feelings of inadequacy to provide for self or the family, and stress from not being able to meet basic needs. A man unable to provide financially for his family can feel inadequate, which leads him to question his manhood. Social stress theory would then argue that a man experiencing this type of stress could become violent because his inability to provide for his family and meet social expectations and obligations makes him feel inadequate. Thus, in this scenario the use of violence becomes a way of asserting and reclaiming manhood. The notion of stress and how it connects to intimate partner violence continues to be examined to frame a dialogue that does not take away from the perpetrator's accountability but does contextualize the violence.

Feminist Theory

Feminist theory asserts that intimate partner violence takes place in a sexist society that is supported by policies and practices that institutionalize women as being subservient to men. Feminist theory states that women's experiences are a result not only of their individual situation, but also of the collective view of women as being lesser than men. Intimate partner violence then becomes a tool men use to reinforce patriarchal institutional structures. The personal is still very much political. The idea that intimate partner violence is used as a mechanism to reinforce patriarchal gender roles is supported by the notion of power and control, which is essentially that men use violence against women as a means of exerting their power over and ability to control them. Perpetrators make the choice to be abusive because the societal structure allows them to and because they live in a society that supports the power and control paradigm. The idea that women continue to experience discrimination is important because it speaks to the larger context of how women can be affected in their relationships. For example, white women continue to earn 77 cents, black women 69 cents, and Latinas 59 cents to the dollar compared with white men. The result of that 25 percent or more loss of salary is that women are less capable of meeting their financial demands. Because women continue to shoulder most of the caregiving responsibilities in the home, that missing 25 percent or more of salary is significant and can render women dependent even when they are working. This example of sexism at a societal level shows how women are affected by systems that superimpose themselves on women's daily lives. Although woman have made important strides that cannot be ignored, they are still confronted with major issues of discrimination and injustice in society that must be addressed if social workers are to better respond to intimate partner violence.

Intersectional Theory

Intersectional theory is increasingly being used in relation to examining issues of violence against women (Lockhart & Danis, 2010; Sokoloff, 2005). Women often lead very complex lives. Intersectional theory asserts that to fully examine violence against women, one has to look at women's multiple layers of life experiences. Intersectional theory examines how race, class, gender, and other forms of oppression and discrimination merge to affect women's experiences related to violence. The idea that multiple layers of oppression affect how women experience violence in their relationships is critical because it provides a more accurate picture of women's lives. Intersectionality also allows practitioners to examine how multiple forms of oppression affect diverse groups of women in relation to intimate partner violence. Intersectional theory challenges the notion that violence against women looks the same regardless of race, class, and other forms of oppression and discrimination. It challenges professionals to consider the idea that intimate partner violence looks different for different women because of the social landscape they are forced to navigate.

For example, women of color not only have to address gender issues, similar to white women, they also have to navigate unique culturally based community expectations and a society that continues to discriminate against people of color. Many women of color do not report abuse out of racial loyalty and the desire and expectation to not bring dishonor and reinforce negative stereotypes of their community. For example, African American and Native American women often choose not to report abuse because of the historical discrimination and violence experienced by both groups at the hands of the criminal justice system. African American women may attempt to protect their partner because of the disproportionate violence and prosecution that African American men have faced in this system. Native American women are often further challenged by law enforcement systems that are nonresponsive and lack understanding of Native culture. Both groups of women face an increased risk of being arrested themselves and having their children removed from the home as a result of intimate partner violence. The issue of immigration is not unique to Latina women; however, many Latina women are forced to navigate systems that are unfriendly and systemically discriminatory toward people with an undocumented immigration status. Reporting intimate partner violence could result in the deportation of both parties and feed into false negative stereotypes of Latinos. Consequently, many Latinas suffer in silence not because they do not know the abuse is wrong, but because of the greater societal oppression they must navigate. Asian women must also navigate the traditions, customs, and laws of their home country that relegate their abuse to silence. If the woman's country of origin has laws and traditions that counter the woman's viability and legal status, then she is governed by those expectations that do not allow her to freely access systems. Multiple forms of oppression are specific not just to race and ethnicity but include sexual orientation, disability status, age, and other issues that intersect to further exacerbate intimate relationship violence. It is important to recognize not only the individual's lived experiences, but also the group's intergenerational experiences; women often make decisions not for themselves but because cultural expectations are strong and support the idea of being silent about abuse. Using intersectional theory will allow practitioners to better examine the complexity of these issues and explore how this complexity affects the choices and decisions made by both the survivor and the perpetrator of abuse.

Afrocentric Theory

Afrocentric theory is a culturally specific framework that emphasizes core ethical principles within communities of African ancestry (Bent-Goodley, 2005). Four essential principles of the Afrocentric paradigm are the need to focus on (1) the role of family structure, community connections, and the subjugation of individual needs to larger familial and community needs; (2) the significance of spirituality as a means of coping with and surviving life challenges; (3) the importance of the oral tradition in comprehending and translating information; and (4) the significance of using rituals to bind groups and contextualize experiences (Gilbert, Harvey,

& Belgrave, 2009; Martin & Martin, 2002; Musgrave, Allen, & Allen, 2002; Schiele, 2000). Specific to domestic violence, one should recognize that the group structure is important to use in interventions as a means of fostering a collective experience, issues of secrecy and placing family and community first are critical to the African American experience, the community must be involved in and viewed as an active and equal partner in program planning and implementation, spirituality is affirmed and recognized as central to programs and services, and building on the oral tradition, different mediums are used to support interventions, such as journaling, poetry, use of music and videos, dance, role playing, and small-group discussions. Thus, Afrocentric theory encourages one to consider how one intervenes with domestic violence, particularly among people of African ancestry.

Myths

Theories have been used to contextualize what causes intimate partner violence. Yet, it is important to identify some of the myths associated with intimate partner violence because people often hold fast to myths regardless of their knowledge of the issue. I want to challenge your ideas of what causes intimate partner violence. Typically, someone will question the idea that these are myths, recounting a situation in which a person reinforced the myth. I further challenge these people because a person's perception of the situation, lack of understanding of intimate partner violence, relationship to the people involved, or desire for the myth to be real often clouds judgment. Consequently, even when armed with information, we must still dispel the myths of why intimate partner abuse exists.

Substance Abuse Causes Intimate Partner Violence

One myth is that substance abuse causes intimate partner violence. Substance abuse does not cause intimate partner violence; however, it has been strongly linked to intimate partner violence and is a significant risk factor that should be taken seriously. Alcohol and drugs have been found in more than one-third of domestic violence cases (Block, 2003). Most offenders who have committed or attempted homicide of an intimate partner were under the influence of alcohol or drugs (Holtzworth-Munroe, Meehan, Herron, Rehman, & Stuart, 2003; Sharps, Campbell, Campbell, Gary, & Webster, 2003). Substance abuse by both the survivor and the perpetrator increases the risk for more lethal and serious injury related to intimate partner violence (Klostermann, Kelley, Mignone, Pusateri, & Fals-Stewart, 2010). Therefore, although substance abuse is not a specific cause of intimate partner violence, it warrants significant attention. The use of alcohol and drugs cannot be dismissed. Women experiencing abuse often use substances as a means of self-medication and a way to escape from the violence. Substance abuse can also be a part of the abusive relationship in which the woman is forced to use the substance or forced to perform sexual acts while under the influence of a substance. More is still being learned about the connection between prescription drug abuse and intimate partner violence. A perpetrator with a substance abuse problem must be treated for both the substance abuse and the perpetration of intimate partner violence (Dalton, 2009; Fenton & Rathus, 2010; Fowler, 2009; Thomas & Bennett, 2009). Yet a person with a substance abuse problem still makes the choice to be abusive and has an awareness of the power and control dynamic. Therefore, the notion that substance abuse causes intimate partner violence is incorrect.

Mental Illness Causes Intimate Partner Violence

The idea that mental illness causes intimate partner violence is also a myth. Poor mental health is connected to intimate partner violence, but it does not cause it. Some perpetrators of abuse have been found to present with antisocial personality disorders. Despite this, the psychopathology does not cause abuse; however, people with psychopathology are often aware of the power and control dynamic. Also, most people with mental illness are not violent toward their partners. Only 10 percent of perpetrators have been diagnosed with a psychiatric disorder, which reinforces the idea that despite mental illness, the person is still making a choice to be abusive. Therefore, the notion that mental illness causes intimate partner violence is incorrect.

The Victim Likes to Be Abused

A sentiment that women like to be abused and, in fact, provoke violence so that they can be abused is common. No one likes to be abused. Nobody wants to be abused. People have some very unhealthy ideas of what constitutes a relationship. However, not having a sense of what qualifies as a healthy relationship and wanting to be abused are two totally different things. When presented with the option, most people would choose to be in a healthy relationship as opposed to an unhealthy one, but that requires knowing the difference between the two and believing that other viable options exist. It is important to understand that women do not want to be abused, and although women may have difficulty getting out of an abusive relationship, it is important to acknowledge that the abuse is not enjoyed or desired. Still, I often hear that women provoke men to be abusive. It is important to note why one could perceive it that way. However, the ultimate decision to be abusive lies with the person who abuses. The idea that the accused perpetrator has little control over making a positive decision or walking away from a situation diminishes his role in and responsibility for the abuse. In addition, the abused partner could have a sense of anticipation, fear, and anxiety that can be interpreted as provocation. It is important to acknowledge and understand that the idea that women enjoy abuse is a myth. Otherwise, social workers can perpetrate, support, and reinforce violence as being acceptable in a relationship.

Only Poor People Experience Intimate Partner Violence

Many myths surround poverty and intimate partner violence. The notion that intimate partner violence only occurs among people in low socioeconomic groups is a myth. Although living in a low-income community increases the risk of experiencing intimate partner violence, violence occurs across all income levels, education levels, employment levels, and class distinctions. Having a high income does not shield someone from experiencing violence or perpetrating violence against a partner. Because of the myth that only poor women experience abuse, some middle-class women may feel a false sense of security and a greater resistance to the idea that they are experiencing intimate partner violence. Social workers must also recognize and distinguish income from wealth, because although income is important, the idea of wealth is also critical, particularly for women of color who are disproportionately less likely to have intergenerational assets and wealth than white women. Some people may have a high income but few assets, which is important because in middle-class communities of color, families' income is often shared with others in the extended family who live in low-income communities. Stretching one's income and diminishing one's wealth limits financial freedom and growth and can create financial problems. So, although a person's income may be high, he or she may still be at economic risk because of these financial obligations and roles. Therefore, income protective factor may not be. Social workers have to better understand how income can be both a protective and a risk factor and how wealth is related to intimate partner violence. Therefore, the idea that only poor people experience intimate partner violence is a myth.

Only People of Color Experience Intimate Partner Violence

The statistics verify that African American and Native American women are at the greatest risk of lethality and serious injury resulting from intimate partner violence (Tjaden & Thoennes, 2000). Yet the idea that domestic violence takes place more often in these communities stems from studies that do not, in my estimation, confirm this assertion. Methodological issues such as small sample sizes, poor methodological approaches, and low reliability and validity of instruments within communities of color all make it difficult to determine that intimate partner violence occurs in communities of color more often than in other communities (Bent-Goodley, 2005). Differential policing in communities of color also makes it challenging to accept this notion. In addition, discrimination in arrest rates in poor communities and communities of color are a factor. Finally, class and geography play a role, in that residential communities with more low-income housing are more likely to have neighbors in close proximity and middle-class communities often have neighbors farther apart from each other, which diminishes neighbors' ability to identify and report abuse. It is important to understand that being a person of color does not mean that one will experience intimate partner violence and that being white does not shield one from experiencing abuse. The risk is there regardless of race and ethnicity. Therefore, the idea that only people of color experience abuse is false.

The Bible Justifies Abuse

The idea that the Bible justifies abuse is also a myth. Some people call on scripture to substantiate or reinforce the idea that men are to dominate their partners and have the moral right and obligation to control them. People pull a scripture from the Bible and point to it as proof that God wants women to be controlled and that abuse is an acceptable method of doing so. However, scripture is often misinterpreted or read discriminately to support a person's perspective, and the scriptures that counter this perspective are not acknowledged. I have always pointed out that the Bible was also used to justify the enslavement of African people, and it is now widely acknowledged that the Bible does not justify the enslavement of any people. However, as one challenges the myth that the Bible justifies the abuse of women, it is important to remember that it was used in this way to support an agenda outside of the doctrine. The idea that the Bible justifies domestic violence is incorrect.

Reflecting Pool

Think about your perceptions of intimate partner violence and what you believe is at the root of it. I believe that this issue is a major one that affects practitioners' ability to work with survivors and perpetrators of abuse. Your perceptions of and what you think is at the root of intimate partner violence will have an impact on how you engage this population. To be able to best serve this population, you must challenge your ideas and where they come from.

My Reflection

I had to examine this issue within myself when I graduated from my MSW program. I had always heard that African American women did not experience intimate partner violence. I heard others say that intimate partner violence was not a black woman's issue but was rather a white woman's issue. The stereotype was that African American women are "superwomen"—strong-willed, able to control any situation, matriarchs who do not tolerate abuse in a relationship. This idea was quickly challenged when I was a new social worker working in the area of child welfare prevention. As I saw the large number of African American women on my caseload struggling with this issue, I had to tackle all of my perceptions and misinformation about intimate partner violence. I challenged myself to reexamine my perceptions, where they came from, and how I could be authentic in my knowledge and attitude. As I challenged myself, I also had to examine why I was comfortable with the myth. Many times, people are invested in a myth for their own reasons. For me, as I gained more knowledge about intimate partner violence, I was forced to recognize my own vulnerability as an African American woman. Once free of the myth, I was empowered to become a better practitioner for my clients. My self-examination allowed me to acknowledge not only that intimate partner violence was happening in the African American community, but also that it was a serious problem.

Your Self Reflection

- Have you ever talked about intimate partner violence and its causes with friends and family?
- What do the people around you think about intimate partner violence?
- Where do your perceptions come from?
- Why do you protect your own myths? What is your investment in the myths?
- What changes when you are honest about the myths?

Notes:

_____
_____
_____
_____
_____
_____
_____
_____
_____
_____
_____
_____
_____

References

Bent-Goodley, T. B. (2005). An African-centered approach to domestic violence. *Families in Society, 86,* 197–206.

Bent-Goodley, T. B. (2009). A black experience-based approach to gender-based violence. *Social Work, 54,* 262–269.

Block, C. (2003). How can practitioners help an abused woman lower her risk of death? *National Institute of Justice Journal, 250,* 4–7.

Corvo, K., Dutton, D., & Wan-Yi, C. (2008). Toward evidence-based practice with domestic violence perpetrators. *Journal of Aggression, Maltreatment & Trauma, 16,* 111–130.

Dalton, B. (2009). Battered program directors' view on substance abuse and domestic violence. *Journal of Aggression, Maltreatment & Trauma, 18,* 248–260.

Fenton, B., & Rathus, J. (2010). Men's self-reported descriptions and precipitants of domestic violence perpetration as reported in intake evaluations. *Journal of Family Violence, 25,* 149–158.

Fowler, D. (2009). Screening for co-occurring intimate partner abuse and substance abuse: Challenges across service delivery system. *Journal of Social Work Practice in the Addictions, 9,* 318–339.

Gilbert, D. J., Harvey, A. R., & Belgrave, F. Z. (2009). Advancing the Africentric paradigm shift discourse: Building toward evidence-based Africentric interventions in social work practice with African Americans. *Social Work, 54,* 243–252.

Hart, S., Dutton, D., & Newlove, T. (1993). The prevalence of personality disorder among wife assaulters. *Journal of Personality Disorders, 7,* 329–341.

Holt, S., Buckley, H., & Whelan, S. (2008). The impact of exposure to domestic violence on children and young people: A review of the literature. *Child Abuse & Neglect, 32,* 797–810.

Holtzworth-Munroe, A., Bates, L., Smutzler, N., & Sandin, E. (1997). A brief review of the research on husband violence Part 1. Maritally violent versus nonviolent men. *Aggressive and Violent Behavior, 2,* 65–99.

Holtzworth-Munroe, A., Meehan, J. C., Herron, K., Rehman, U., & Stuart, G. L. (2003). Do subtypes of maritally violent men continue to differ over time? *Journal of Consulting and Clinical Psychology, 71,* 728.

Holtzworth-Munroe, A., Stuart, G. L., & Hutchinson, G. (1997). Violent versus nonviolent husbands: Differences in attachment patterns, dependency, and jealousy. *Journal of Family Psychology, 11,* 314–331.

Klostermann, K., Kelley, M. L., Mignone, T., Pusateri, L., & Fals-Stewart, W. (2010). Partner violence and substance abuse: Treatment interventions. *Aggression and Violent Behavior, 15,* 162–166.

Lockhart, L., & Danis, F. (Eds.). (2010). *Domestic violence: Intersectionality and culturally competent practice.* New York: Columbia University Press.

Martin, E. P., & Martin, J. M. (2002). *Spirituality and the black helping tradition in social work.* Washington, DC: NASW Press.

Musgrave, C. F., Allen, C. E., & Allen, G. J. (2002). Spirituality and health for women of color. *American Journal of Public Health, 92,* 557–560.

Ornduff, S. R., Kelsey, R. M., & O'Leary, D. (2001). Childhood physical abuse, personality, and adult relationship violence: A model of vulnerability. *American Journal of Orthopsychiatry, 71,* 322–331.

Pears, K., & Capaldi, D. (2001). Intergenerational transmission of abuse: A two-generational prospective study of an at-risk sample. *Child Abuse & Neglect, 25,* 1439–1461.

Potter, H. (2008). *Battle cries: Black women and intimate partner abuse.* New York: New York University Press.

Schiele, J. (2000). *Human services and the Afrocentric paradigm.* New York: Haworth Press.

Sharps, P., Campbell, J., Campbell, D., Gary, F., & Webster, D. (2003). Risky mix: Drinking, drug use, and homicide. *NIJ Journal, 250,* 8–13.

Sokoloff, N. (2005). *Domestic violence at the margins: Readings on race, class, gender, and culture.* New Brunswick, NJ: Rutgers University Press.

Thomas, M., & Bennett, L. (2009). The co-occurrence of substance abuse and domestic violence: A comparison of dual-problem men in substance abuse treatment and in a court-ordered batterer program. *Journal of Social Work Practice in the Addictions, 9,* 299–317.

Tjaden, P., & Thoennes, N. (2000). *Extent, nature and consequences of violence against women: Findings from the National Violence Against Women Survey* (NCJ 181867). Washington, DC: Bureau of Justice Statistics.

Walker, L. (2006). Violence and exploitation against women and girls. *Annals of the New York Academy of Sciences, 1087,* 142–157.

Wareham, J., Boots, D. P., & Chavez, J. M. (2009). A test of social learning and intergenerational transmission among batterers. *Journal of Criminal Justice, 37,* 163–173.

Select Resources

- *Battered Women's Shelter of Summit and Medina Counties:* http://www. scmcbws.org/myths_facts.asp

- *Domesticviolence.org:* http://www.domesticviolence.org/common-myths/

- *Faith Trust Institute:* http://www.faithtrustinstitute.org

- *Michigan Victim Assistance Academy:* http://www.cj.msu.edu/~outreach/mvaa/

- *National Online Resource Center on Violence Against Women:* http://www. vawnet.org/

- *University of Minnesota Human Rights Library:* http://www1.umn.edu/humanrts/svaw/domestic/link/theories.htm

Three

Why Does She Stay?

In this chapter, I focus on answering the questions that I hear most often: "Why does she stay?" "Why would she put herself in this type of situation?" "What is wrong with her for putting up with this?" These questions place significant judgment against the survivor and at times seem almost accusatory or blaming the survivor for the abuse (Thapar-Bjorkert & Morgan, 2010). At other times, they reflect disbelief that a person would perpetrate violence toward an intimate partner. The questions also imply that the survivor can control the violence she is experiencing. Still, these questions serve as valuable representations of how people think about intimate partner violence. So, consider this chapter an opportunity to explore your thinking as to why she stays.

Cycle of Abuse

The cycle of abuse is an important tool that allows women to put what they are experiencing individually into a broader context. It focuses largely on three stages: (1) the honeymoon stage, (2) the tension-building stage, and (3) the abusive incident. From my perspective, the cycle of abuse has some additional dynamics that warrant being highlighted and teased out to

Figure 3-1: Cycle of Abuse

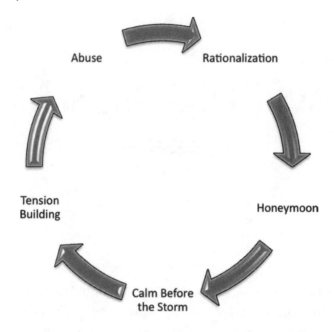

more fully understand the cycle, so I have added two additional stages—the rationalization stage and the calm-before-the-storm stage.

As a practitioner, I use the cycle of abuse as a tool with survivors for two reasons: (1) to help them understand that they are not in this alone because countless other women have experienced domestic violence—enough for researchers to have generated a cycle that, in most cases, represents what survivors experience—and (2) to give them the opportunity to identify what, in fact, they are experiencing. It allows survivors to understand that what they are experiencing is predictable and part of a cycle. In some ways, as survivors become aware of the cycle of abuse, they begin to see what they are experiencing not just as an individual experience but also as a collective experience. I have always been reminded that a woman leaves a relationship upwards of seven to eight times before finally leaving and not returning to the relationship. Consequently, women are at greatest risk when they leave the relationship. In addition, a woman's risk of experiencing serious injury and lethality increases when she leaves the relationship as the perpetrator attempts to regain control over her (Catlett, Toews, & Walilko, 2010; Fenton & Rathus, 2010). Understanding these facts has allowed me not to personalize when a woman does not leave the relationship but instead be reminded of the cycle and the risks associated with the violence.

The cycle of abuse does not just serve as a means to inform the practitioner; if used properly, it can help a woman make different choices, find new solutions, and empower herself to create change and understand the nature of her choices. The other function of the cycle of abuse is to help build a connection between the woman and other survivors. Part of the challenge of intimate partner violence is that the perpetrator is able to isolate the survivor, and so the cycle of abuse is a tool to help her realize that she is really not alone. It can also help the survivor understand the cycle and gain a more informed sense of the patterns of abuse in the relationship. So the cycle of abuse is not just something to give to a survivor with a limited explanation. Instead, it can be used to help the survivor identify the patterns in a relationship, acknowledge that she is a part of something bigger than herself, and realize that she has opportunities and can safely make other choices.

Something important to remember is that the cycle of abuse is not happening between two people who do not know each other; rather, it takes place in the context of a relationship, which means that the woman has an investment in the person and in the relationship. This investment makes it difficult to just walk away from the relationship. The woman may have a sense of commitment to the relationship and want to see it work. Although she does not like the abuse, she may still genuinely love the person or who the person used to be and hope that he will revert back to who he once was. In some respects, she may be grieving the loss of the relationship and the person she felt she knew in that relationship. I want to emphasize that understanding and working through these emotions and thinking takes time. Putting the cycle into this context allows practitioners to put aside their feelings about the relationship and instead understand that the abuse is taking place in the context of the relationship's history.

Rationalization

In the rationalization stage, there is denial of the abuse, not only by the perpetrator, but also by the survivor. This stage is important because the woman often has a feeling that something is wrong with the relationship. During this phase, the woman may not necessarily know that she is experiencing abuse, but she may have a sense of uncertainty and doubt about what is taking place in the relationship and begin to question her instinct that something is wrong with it. Friends and family may also express concerns about the relationship. She may feel that the person can change and that she can help him change. She may also think that she triggered the problems in the relationship. The rationalization stage is important because it is a period of time in which the woman feels some sense of doubt in the relationship. The moment in which the woman questions herself is very powerful. The woman may, at some point, begin to feel a sense of betrayal—that she has betrayed her thoughts, her instincts, or advice given by friends and family. So social workers need to acknowledge this stage and create opportunities for discussion and support around the woman's rationalization.

Honeymoon Stage

The honeymoon stage occurs at the point at which the perpetrator expresses remorse for the abuse. During this stage, the man is being who the woman wants him to be and who he may have been at the beginning of the relationship. In this stage, the perpetrator may be apologetic. He says all of the right things, which can be very confusing for the woman because in the previous stage, she had a sense of doubt about the relationship. The honeymoon stage capitalizes on that moment and essentially highlights the perpetrator's manipulation by telling the woman what she wants to hear. During this stage, the perpetrator is good at giving the woman a sense of comfort and ease that nothing else is going to happen. He creates an environment that allows the woman to lower her defenses and believe that he will not continue to be abusive. This stage is very challenging for family and friends because, again, the perpetrator is doing and saying all the right things. It is important for those around the woman to understand what is happening in this stage. This stage can be very frustrating for those around the survivor because it is difficult to counter her emotions, the perpetrator's actions, and the frustration of seeing her revert to a feeling of false security or doubt about walking away from the relationship. It is important to remember that this is a stage, and knowing that, social workers can understand movement from the stage will occur in time.

Calm Before the Storm

After the honeymoon stage, people often go straight to the tension-building stage. However, I believe that it is important to acknowledge that, many times, before one gets to the tension-building stage, a sense of regularity and calm is present in the relationship and the violence is not uppermost in the survivor's mind. During this stage, the perpetrator is on his best behavior, which is confusing and challenging for the survivor because she is trying to understand what is happening. I liken this period of time to the calm before the storm. It can be uneventful, and so the woman gains a sense of regularity, ease, and normalcy. She then feels more relaxed in the relationship and is lulled into a false sense of security that the problem has been resolved. During this stage, she lets her guard down and characterizes the violence as a particular incident or the result of something she did wrong. She may even attribute the violence to something that happened to the man but disregard the abuse as a pattern of behavior. This calmness makes the next stage that much more confusing.

Tension-building Stage

The tension-building stage is often likened to the feeling of walking on egg shells. In this stage, the woman begins to feel a sense of uneasiness and that something is going to happen, but she does not know when or how or the circumstances surrounding it. In this stage, many things can occur. For example, the woman may try to do everything she can to avoid an abusive incident. In this regard, she may be doing all that the perpetrator asks of her in an effort to avoid the abuse. She also has no idea what the length of time will be between abusive incidents and feels powerless to stop it from occurring. During this very challenging stage, some women choose to find ways to diminish the potential for an abusive incident to occur, and then feel anxious in such a way that they try to get the abusive incident behind them. Some may think that the women provoked the violence. Yet, the survivor, in effect, be trying to find some way to control the situation. It is important to be able to discern this behavior from provocation in the way that people have become accustomed to understanding it. For some women, it is an opportunity to get past the fear, anxiety, and anticipation of the abuse, which can be disabling. It is important for social workers to understand that they could misread what is happening as provocation rather than what it really is—an attempt to control a situation that she cannot control.

Abusive Incident

The next stage is the abusive incident. I talk about what constitutes abuse shortly, but it is important to remember that women can go through these stages in and out of cyclical order. In addition, abusive incidents occur in no specific time frame. For some women, abuse can happen every day or multiple times a day. For other women, abuse may take place every year during a particular time period, or incidents may occur years apart. Regardless of the time between stages of the cycle, in most cases, if a man is abusive, then he will be abusive again. The other point to remember is that the order in which the stages occur can be different for each person. For example, for some survivors, abuse takes place progressively over a period of time in the relationship. For others, the abuse begins relatively early in the relationship and becomes worse over time. These complexities are important to understand to put the cycle of abuse in context and use it as an optimal tool for working with survivors.

Dimensions of Intimate Partner Violence

So what is intimate partner violence? The power and control wheel is often used to provide a visual representation of domestic violence. The power and control wheel provides a visual representation of physical, sexual, psychology, and economic abuse.

The power and control wheel is most often used to highlight the components of abuse. I have found that understanding domestic violence often requires you to put the pieces of a larger puzzle together. At times, you are searching to put information into context and understand how or even if the information connects with intimate partner violence. Many clients do not necessarily state that they are experiencing intimate partner violence, so the practitioner must be able to put the pieces of the puzzle together deliberately and conscientiously.

Physical Abuse

Physical abuse includes the things that people initially think about when they think of intimate partner violence, such as hitting, shaking, grabbing, kicking, punching, slapping, pushing, shoving, choking, burning, and shooting. However, physical abuse also includes withholding medicine from or denying medical care to a person and forcing a person to use drugs and alcohol.

Recognizing that how one defines an issue is important, practitioners must remember to ask their clients how they define domestic violence. Language and definitions are key to avoiding miscommunication. For example, one study found a group of African American women who considered pushing and shoving not as an indication of intimate partner violence but instead as a means of working out conflict in a relationship (Bent-Goodley, 2004). They further shared that they considered domestic violence to have occurred if a beating resulted in blood or broken bones; however, bruises and scrapes as a result of abuse were not considered domestic violence. These perceptions are not true of all African American women. However, they represent the view of a group of women. It is important that practitioners ask clients about their definition of physical abuse and understand some of the perceptions of physical abuse within the community. Otherwise, they could miss opportunities to intervene and provide support and information.

Examples of Physical Abuse

- hitting
- pushing
- shoving
- burning
- shaking
- slapping
- kicking
- grabbing
- withholding medication or medical services
- forcing the use of drugs or alcohol

Sexual Abuse

Sexual abuse occurs in close to half of relationships in which domestic violence occurs (Campbell & Soeken, 1999; Campbell et al., 2003). Almost 8 million women have been raped by an intimate partner (National Center for Injury Prevention and Control, 2003). Sexual abuse includes acts such as forcing sex, forcing the person to engage in sex with other people, forcing the person

to engage in sexual acts against his or her will or in ways that are uncomfortable for him or her, forcing a person to have sex for material items, having other people watch sexual acts, forcing a person to use drugs while having sex, forcing a person to have sex without protection, forcing someone to become pregnant, and forcing someone to terminate a pregnancy. These examples of sexual abuse are critical pieces of the puzzle to understand and be aware of when responding to domestic violence. A question I have often been asked is, "If my partner is withholding sex from me, is that a form of sexual abuse"? Withholding sex can be a form of sexual abuse. However, once again, it must be taken in context. Not having sex on demand in a relationship is not sexual abuse. Not having sex for a length of time because of just not wanting to have sex or problems with intimacy, health, or other issues within the relationship is not sexual abuse. The intent behind withholding sex, along with other indicators in the relationship, is key to understanding.

Examples of Sexual Abuse

- forcing sex
- forcing sex in exchange for items
- forcing sex with multiple people
- forcing the person to engage in sexual acts
- forcing the person to use drugs while having sex
- forcing someone to become pregnant

Economic Abuse

When people think about economic abuse, they often envision a person being denied financial support to meet basic human needs. This example of economic abuse is correct; however, it is only one example. Economic abuse also includes acts such as taking someone's financial resources, preventing a person from being able to get or retain employment,

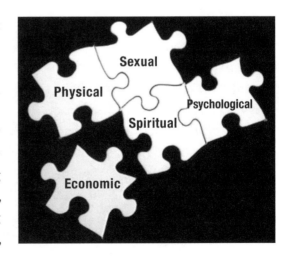

providing insufficient financial support to meet basic human needs, or keeping financial and other resources away from a person. Another example often not considered to be part of economic abuse is using immigration status to withhold resources and supports and threatening to report immigration status as a means of controlling the partner. Some people believe that economic abuse is primarily seen in low-income populations; however, middle-class, professional women also struggle with not being able to control their finances because a perpetrator has assumed control over financial resources in the home. In some cases, no physical or sexual abuse may be taking place; however, using economic abuse as a tool to control a woman is powerful and requires identification and attention.

Examples of Economic Abuse

- taking someone's financial resources, income, and assets
- withholding basic human needs
- preventing a person from attaining or maintaining employment
- preventing a person from attaining or completing education
- withholding financial and other resources
- threatening immigration status

Psychological Abuse

Psychological abuse includes the verbal, emotional, and mental ways in which the perpetrator attempts to control the survivor. It is a concept often identified but not as well measured in domestic violence research and practice (Follingstad, 2007). Yet, although bruises and scars may heal, the wounds of psychological abuse often remain long after the visible

signs of abuse are gone. Psychological abuse includes many things, such as verbal abuse through name calling, putting the person down, diminishing the person and his or her accomplishments or potential, telling a person that no one else wants him or her, being overly possessive, isolating the person from others, making threats, intimidating the person, and playing mind games.

Isolation

A survivor can be isolated from friends and family by moving him or her out of the physical environment, but a survivor can also be isolated by creating tension in the woman's relationships and creating an environment in which friends and family become frustrated and withdraw from the relationship because of the ongoing abuse. Isolating the survivor is a powerful technique because it removes supports, resources, and the feeling of having options outside of the relationship. It compounds feelings of emotional abuse by creating a feeling of being disconnected and alone.

Coercion and Threats

Coercion and threats are additional forms of psychological abuse. Many perpetrators make threats and use coercion to control the survivor. Threats to hurt or kill a child, family member, or pet or even to commit suicide are all strategies used to control the survivor. The connection to animal abuse is very important and must be considered part of assessment and treatment (Becker & French, 2004; Faver & Strand, 2003; Randour, 2007; Robbins, 2006). In fact, 60 percent of people who witnessed or perpetrated animal abuse have been found to have reported domestic violence or child maltreatment as a child (DeGue & DiLillo, 2009). Thus, threats of animal abuse often progress into criminal acts against pets, which must be taken seriously. Destroying property, such as punching holes in the wall or slamming objects, is used to make the survivor think about what can happen to her. Another way of manipulating the survivor into staying in the relationship is to make her feel that she is a bad parent and threaten to make false reports to child protective services. Perpetrators are becoming more aware of how to use psychological abuse without making threats so they can avoid legal consequences for this type of abuse. Practitioners must be aware of this so that this dimension is not unidentified or minimized.

Psychological abuse can be likened to a war for the mind. It is part of creating an imprint in the person's mind that plays over and over, creating a mental prison regardless of whether the perpetrator is present. Thus, the woman experiences a very real perception of fear and risk. Although the practitioner may not know or understand how this imprint is instilled into the woman's thinking, that it makes it very difficult for the woman to walk away and leave the relationship is clear. Social workers have to work hard to understand the imprint and find creative, effective ways to help the woman dismantle it, create a new inner map to guide her thinking, and heal.

Examples of Psychological Abuse

- verbally abusing the person
- minimizing the person
- blaming the person for the violence
- playing tricks and mind games
- controlling the person
- using threats and coercion
- isolating the person
- putting the person down
- threatening to abuse animals and pets
- threatening to abuse the children or other family members and friends
- threatening to commit suicide
- threatening to kill the person

Spiritual Abuse

I believe that acknowledging spiritual abuse as its own separate dimension is vital because although it is not fully evident in the other forms of abuse, it is critical for many women struggling with violence. For many women, the spiritual connection is powerful and can affect and be affected by intimate partner violence. Spiritual abuse is revealed by activities such as using religion and religious doctrine as a tool to manipulate the survivor, denying the survivor the ability to worship and practice her faith, isolating the woman from her faith community, using members of the faith-based community to support the violent relationship, using religious doctrine such as

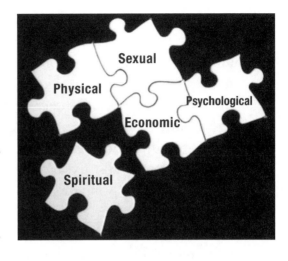

the focus on forgiveness and positions against divorce to keep the person in the abusive relationship, and creating doubt in the survivor's mind about a higher power's ability to change her situation (Bent-Goodley & Fowler, 2006; Dehan & Levi, 2009; Lyon, 2010).

Spirituality and religion are different (Bent-Goodley, 2006; Martin & Martin, 2002). Religion focuses on the ways a person practices his or her faith, such as regular attendance at a faith-based community, reading religious doctrine, and attending faith-based events. Spirituality includes prayer and belief in a higher power and speaks to belief in and perceived connection to that higher power. Understanding this type of abuse is important to understanding people who use spirituality as a coping mechanism and protective factor to advance spiritual well-being (Bent-Goodley & Fowler, 2006; Nason-Clark, 2004, 2010). Spiritual and religious beliefs can be used to cope with the violence experienced, determine when and how to seek support, aid in deciding to leave the perpetrator, reinforce that the violence is not acceptable, and provide a sense of hope and existence that transcends the situation (Bent-Goodley, 2007; Hassouneh-Phillips, 2003; Nason-Clark, 2004; Watlington & Murphy, 2006; Wendt, 2008; West, 1999). Spirituality goes beyond how a person thinks or feels. It reflects how a person finds hope in a situation or believes in the possible when someone else sees only impossibilities. "Psychological abuse is more cognitive. Spirituality speaks to the foundation of your being, the essence of who you are" (Bent-Goodley & Fowler, 2006, p. 290). Women of color are more likely than white women to turn to their faith and faith-based community for support than to social workers, law enforcement, and other professional groups (Hampton & Gullotta, 2006; Watlington & Murphy, 2006). Faith-based groups can increase help seeking, use of resources, and use of religious problem solving; reinforce safety plans and intervention outcomes; and address religious teachings about gender and gender roles (Wang, Horne, Levitt, & Klesges, 2009). Faith-based providers are also more likely than formal providers to understand the family history and generational context of the violence, which can be key to assisting the person (Moon & Shim, 2010). Therefore, practitioners have to understand the role of spirituality in intimate partner violence and develop the ability to engage and work with faith-based communities to respond to domestic violence.

Examples of Spiritual Abuse

- using and manipulating holy scripture to justify intimate partner violence
- keeping the person from attending religious services and activities
- using religious doctrine, such as the principle of forgiveness, to reinforce staying in an abusive relationship
- isolating the person from the faith community
- creating doubt in the survivor's mind as to the higher power's ability to stop the violence
- removing or destroying religious articles
- denying the person the ability to engage actively in religious practices

Reflecting Pool

In this chapter, I explored reasons why women stay in abusive relationships, the cycle of violence, and dimensions of domestic violence to help put the pieces of the puzzle together. I hope it has given you an opportunity to understand not just the cycle of abuse but the many ways in which abuse can occur. In the Reflecting Pool, I challenge you to consider your thinking about why survivors stay in relationships.

My Reflection

I remember the first client whom I helped to acquire sufficient out-of-state transportation and leave her abusive partner. I was so excited that I had mastered and used such strong advocacy skills to obtain the resources she needed to change her life and the lives of her children. When she did not show up at our agreed-on time to leave, I was upset and frustrated. It took so much for me to get the resources to assist her. I was also confused because she seemed so strongly set on leaving, and I had invested significant time in helping her get to that place. I later found out that she became afraid and decided not to leave. As a new practitioner, I became frustrated with this scenario, especially after experiencing it several times from the same and different women. As a more informed practitioner, I learned to praise women for their courage to consider leaving and for their strength in navigating their situation. I had to remind myself that their courage was considerable, realizing that they were the ones enduring the realities of their situation. Putting into effect what I learned about the cycle of abuse, the dimensions of domestic violence, how often women try to leave an abusive relationship, and the dire risk they take when they do leave has helped me to think less about the time I have invested and my frustration with the situation and more about helping to support women on their journey.

Your Reflection

- Why do you think women stay in abusive relationships?
- Where do your ideas come from?
- Have you ever felt as though the challenges survivors experience are because of their actions? Think it through.
- Do you feel that women do provoke violence?

- What myths do you have about domestic violence?
- How do you define domestic violence and how does that affect your work?
- What are your thoughts on the dimensions of domestic violence? Do you value some thoughts more than others? Explain your thinking.

Notes:

_____
_____
_____
_____
_____
_____
_____
_____
_____
_____
_____
_____

References

Becker, F., & French, L. (2004). Making the links: Child abuse, animal cruelty, and domestic violence. *Child Abuse Review, 13,* 399–414.

Bent-Goodley, T. B. (2004). Perceptions of domestic violence: A dialogue with African American women. *Health & Social Work, 29,* 307–316.

Bent-Goodley, T. B. (2006). Domestic violence and the black church: Challenging abuse one soul at a time. In R. L. Hampton & T. P. Gullotta (Eds.), *Interpersonal violence in the African-American community: Evidence-based prevention and treatment practices* (pp. 107–119). New York: Springer.

Bent-Goodley, T. B. (2007). Health disparities and violence against women. *Trauma, Violence & Abuse, 8,* 90–104.

Bent-Goodley, T., & Fowler, D. N. (2006). Spiritual and religious abuse. *Affilia: Journal of Women and Social Work, 21,* 282–292.

Campbell, J., & Soeken, K. (1999). Forced sex and intimate partner violence: Effects on women's risk and women's health. *Violence Against Women, 5,* 1017–1035.

Campbell, J., Webster, D., Koziol-McLain, J., Block, C., Campbell, D., Curry, M., et al. (2003). Risk factors for femicide in abusive relationships: Results from a multisite case control study. *American Journal of Public Health, 93,* 1089–1097.

Catlett, B., Toews, M., & Walilko, V. (2010). Men's gendered constructions of intimate partner violence as predictors of court-mandated batterer treatment drop out. *American Journal of Community Psychology, 45,* 107–123.

DeGue, S., & DiLillo, D. (2009). Is animal cruelty a "red flag" for family violence? Investigating co-occurring violence towards children, partners, and pets. *Journal of Interpersonal Violence, 24,* 1036–1056.

Dehan, N., & Levi, Z. (2009). Spiritual abuse: An additional dimension of abuse experienced by abused Haredi (Ultraorthodox) Jewish wives. *Violence Against Women, 15,* 1294–1310.

Faver, S., & Strand, E. (2003). Domestic violence and animal cruelty: Untangling the web of abuse. *Journal of Social Work Education, 39,* 237–254.

Fenton, B., & Rathus, J. (2010). Men's self-reported descriptions and precipitants of domestic violence perpetration as reported in intake evaluations. *Journal of Family Violence, 25,* 149–158.

Follingstad, D. R. (2007). Rethinking current approaches to psychological abuse: Conceptual and methodological issues. *Aggression & Violent Behavior, 12,* 439–458.

Hampton, R. L., & Gullotta, T. P. (2006). *Interpersonal violence in the African-American community: Evidence-based prevention and treatment practices.* New York: Springer.

Hassouneh-Phillips, D. (2003). Strength and vulnerability: Spirituality in abused American Muslim women's lives. *Issues in Mental Health Nursing, 24,* 681–694.

Lyon, E. (2010). The spiritual implications of interpersonal abuse: Speaking of the soul. *Pastoral Psychology, 59,* 233–247.

Martin, E. P., & Martin, J. M. (2002). *Spirituality and the black helping tradition in social work*. Washington, DC: NASW Press.

Moon, S., & Shim, W. (2010). Bridging pastoral counseling and social work practice: An exploratory study of pastors' perceptions of and responses to intimate partner violence. *Journal of Religion & Spirituality in Social Work, 29,* 124–142.

Nason-Clark, N. (2004). When terror strikes home: The interface between religion and domestic violence. *Journal for the Scientific Study of Religion, 43,* 303–310.

Nason-Clark, N. (2010). *No place for abuse: Biblical and practical resources to counteract domestic violence*. Downers Grove, IL: InterVarsity Press.

National Center for Injury Prevention and Control. (2003). *Costs of intimate partner violence against women in the United States*. Atlanta: Author.

Randour, M. (2007). Integrating animals into the family violence paradigm: Implications for policy and professional standards. *Journal of Emotional Abuse, 7,* 97–116.

Robbins, J. (2006). Recognizing the relationship between domestic violence and animal abuse: Recommendations for change to the Texas legislature. *Texas Journal of Women and the Law, 16,* 129–147.

Thapar-Bjorkert, S., & Morgan, K. (2010). "But sometimes I think . . . they put themselves in the situation": Exploring blame and responsibility in interpersonal violence. *Violence Against Women, 16,* 32–59.

Wang, M. C., Horne, S., Levitt, H., & Klesges, L. (2009). Christian women in IPV relationships: An exploratory study of religious factors. *Journal of Psychology and Christianity, 28,* 224–235.

Watlington, C. G., & Murphy, C. M. (2006). The roles of religion and spirituality among African American survivors of domestic violence. *Journal of Clinical Psychology, 62,* 837–857.

Wendt, S. (2008). Christianity and domestic violence. *Affilia: Journal of Women and Social Work, 23,* 144–155.

West, T. C. (1999). *Wounds of the spirit: Black women, violence, and resistance ethics*. New York: New York University Press.

Select Resources

- *The Black Church and Domestic Violence Institute:* http://www.bcdvi.org/thisfarbyfaith.cfm
- *Domestic Violence Awareness Project:* http://dvam.vawnet.org/
- *National Coalition Against Domestic Violence:* http://www.ncadv.org
- *Rape, Abuse, and Incest National Network:* http://www.rainn.org/
- *State Domestic Violence Coalitions:* http://www.ovw.usdoj.gov/statedomestic.htm
- *State Sexual Assault Coalitions:* http://www.ovw.usdoj.gov/statesexual.htm

Four

Signs and Lethality of Intimate Partner Violence

Now that you understand what constitutes domestic violence, I will focus on signs indicating that domestic violence may be taking place and lethality factors related to domestic violence. These signs are opportunities for professionals to address domestic violence before it progresses to more serious or lethal violence. These signs should not be used in a prescriptive fashion and could be a sign of an unhealthy relationship but not necessarily an abusive one. Practitioners have to take all of this information into context and look at all of the patterns and issues as they consider signs of abuse and lethality factors. Each of these signs provides professionals with an opportunity to assess the relationship so that they can better understand what is happening.

It is important to realize that even though one may not always recognize the signs of abuse, some signs are typically manifested at different stages in a relationship. It is important to acknowledge these signs for what they are. One sign in and of itself may not constitute abuse, but if a practitioner sees several of these indicators, he or she has a better view to put the pieces of the puzzle together. I discuss these indicators in three ways: (1) what the survivor is experiencing, (2) what the perpetrator is doing, and (3) what others may be witnessing.

Are You in an Abusive Relationship?

- Is your partner controlling?
- Is your partner possessive?
- Is your partner jealous and accusatory?
- Does your partner use abusive language toward you?
- Does your partner blame you for his or her behavior?
- Does your partner threaten to harm him- or herself?
- Does your partner threaten to harm you?
- Does your partner threaten to harm the children or your family?
- Does your partner threaten to harm your pet?
- Does your partner touch you in a way that you are not comfortable with physically or sexually?

Controlling Behavior

Controlling a partner's behavior or having one's behavior controlled by a partner is a key indicator of intimate partner violence. Controlling what a person wears, whom the person can talk to, and where a person can go and when are all indicators of an abusive relationship. Isolating the person from friends and family by alienating him or her from networks, creating a hostile or uncomfortable environment, or moving him or her outside of his or her geographic support network are all key indicators. Taking the person away from his or her support system and natural environment further alienates him or her. It could start with the perpetrator filling the survivor's head with the idea that family and friends are jealous of her and attempting to destroy the relationship. This sentiment increases the woman's becoming alienated and progressively disconnected from her support system both physically and emotionally. Once this occurs, the woman has even more difficulty reaching out to others for support. She may recognize that her circle is getting smaller and smaller and her supports are decreasing, which is a clear signal of isolation and that she is possibly in an abusive relationship. Friends may find the person is increasingly unavailable, or they may feel uncomfortable or tense in the presence of the couple or the perpetrator. These are signs to look for within and outside of the relationship.

Possessiveness

Some women associate possessiveness with love. They think that when a man is possessive or controlling, he is showing the intensity of his love. It is important to understand when being possessive is an indicator of an abusive relationship. If the man does not allow his partner to be around or interact with other people, then his concern is unhealthy and is often an indicator of abuse. Constantly calling, controlling where and when she goes places, hiding messages from others, or not allowing others to interact with the woman are all signs of an unhealthy relationship and, in many cases, of an abusive one. However, if the man does not try to control his partner or his partner's behavior but instead expresses a concern for her safety and well-being, then that is not an indicator. These distinctions are very important to understand because in the first case the woman is being controlled by the man's concern but in the second case, the man is simply expressing a concern.

Jealousy

Jealousy is another indicator of intimate partner violence and is not indicative of a healthy relationship. The man may be jealous of the woman's relationships with friends, family, people in the workplace, or even people in a place of worship. The man could also be jealous of the woman because she is employed, attending school, or having success in the workplace or her career. The jealousy may initially be expressed as concern for the woman but becomes progressively worse, with expectations and demands being enforced. The perpetrator may move from articulating negative messages to stalking the woman, forcing others to disengage from her, sabotaging her at work or school, destroying property, or trying to make her feel bad about her accomplishments. All are indicators of abuse. When jealousy moves to controlling the person's ability to interact with others or to achieve, then it is a clear sign of abuse.

Abusive Language or Verbal Abuse

Another important indicator of abuse is verbal abuse, which includes belittling the woman, calling her names, putting her down, telling her that she will never be good enough, and embarrassing her. It is important to understand verbal abuse. Some people feel that for domestic violence to be present, some physical abuse must have occurred, when, in fact, a person's entire relationship could be verbally and emotionally abusive with no physical abuse. This abuse is still considered domestic violence. Although it may not fit the legal definition of domestic violence, it is a critical form of abuse focused solely on diminishing and controlling the person. It allows the perpetrator to create an environment in which the survivor begins to question herself and wonder whether the negative things the man is saying are true. This dynamic creates real challenges from an emotional standpoint; the woman has to try to maneuver out of this web of confusion that has been created intentionally to control her. Those looking in from outside of the relationship should recognize the verbal abuse as a sign of domestic violence. Also, perpetrators are becoming more sophisticated in how they use verbal abuse. Because making threats is a crime in many states and can be prosecuted, many perpetrators are being verbally abusive but are not making threats, to avoid arrest. Consequently, practitioners must be that much more vigilant in observing what is occurring in the relationship.

Blame Game

Another important sign of an abusive relationship is when the perpetrator blames the survivor for the abuse. So, for example, the perpetrator will blame the survivor for the abusive incident or problems in the relationship and accept little to no responsibility for his actions. He may say the woman provoked him by not doing what she was told, by expressing her opinion, or because of her personal shortcomings. To justify the abuse, he may say that something about her is lacking or insufficient. The perpetrator will fault the survivor for the choices he has made to be abusive. This blame game can become very confusing to the survivor who may, over time, begin to wonder whether the blame is suitable. Friends may find the woman making excuses for the behavior or justifying and rationalizing the violence. Practitioners must be able to point out these contradictions and affirm the woman.

Threats and Threatening Behavior

Threatening to harm himself, the survivor, a friend, a family member, a child, or a pet are all examples of abuse, so it is important to recognize that a person's threatening the well-being of people or animals is a major red flag that abuse is present. In addition to verbal threats, the perpetrator may also use threatening physical behaviors. For example, he may punch a hole in the wall or destroy personal property. All of this is done to make the survivor consider what can happen to her or people she cares about. Making threats is a way to control the woman's behavior and thinking, essentially because she is afraid and becomes more easily controlled through her fear. Although the people around her may not believe the man is going to carry out the threat, the threats are powerful and real to the woman living in the situation. Practitioners and those who want to help must have patience and take these threats seriously. They must remember that the woman is trying to survive and maintain her safety and perhaps that of her children. These threats are not arbitrary. They are real, and professionals have to put the necessary precautions in place to enhance the woman's safety. Understanding how threats are used is important in assisting the survivor.

Physical and Sexual Violence

Another important sign of abuse is physical and sexual violence. Although I have talked about them as types of violence, it is important to acknowledge them as signs of domestic violence because some people think that some forms of physical abuse are acceptable in a relationship. Physical violence is never an acceptable or healthy way to resolve conflicts in a relationship. I want to also remind you that physical abuse can take place over different periods of time. I have often been asked, "If it happens only once, does that make it abuse?" My first response is, "How do you know it will only happen once?" In most cases of abuse, it takes place more than once.

The chances of the abuse recurring are even stronger if the perpetrator has not taken responsibility for his actions and obtained treatment, although his doing so does not guarantee that he will not be abusive in the future. Sexual abuse is another important sign. Any time a woman is forced to have sex, forced to commit sexual acts, forced to have sex with people with whom she does not want to have sex, or forced to have unprotected sex, then she is being sexually abused. It is important to unlock one's stereotypes and think about what constitutes sexual abuse because how it can be experienced varies. Both physical and sexual abuse are clear indicators that one is in an abusive relationship.

Additional Indicators

Some of the signs of domestic abuse may not be easily visible. However, both the person being abused and the abuser often show signs that are clear indicators of abuse. I believe that women often sense or have a feeling that something is wrong in the relationship, and I encourage them to trust themselves and their intuition. More than likely, if a woman thinks she is in an abusive relationship, then she is in an abusive relationship. I encourage women to trust their gut feelings and reactions, and call the abuse what it is. A woman may be afraid of her partner, afraid to bring up certain topics, afraid to share her feelings, or afraid to speak up about issues in the relationship. She may be afraid of what will happen to her for speaking out. She may question herself, how she ended up in the situation, and the role she played in the problem. Practitioners who see a woman going back and forth in her thinking about what she is experiencing should take the opportunity to encourage her to trust in what she inherently knows but is not allowing herself to fully accept.

Another important indicator is when the woman begins to feel emotionally numb. At this point, the woman may just check out of the relationship because of her feelings of being hopeless, helpless, powerless, and unable to change the situation. Most women who experience abuse likely feel this detachment. Some women experience it for a short period of time and others experience it for a much longer period of time, but in any event not feeling like they can change the situation can lead to their becoming emotionally detached from people in their life.

These feelings have a cognitive, emotional, and spiritual impact on women. They are powerful mechanisms that further control women's actions. At a minimum, they are a reflection of being in an unhealthy relationship; however, they can also be indicators of being in a domestic violence situation.

Lethality Indicators

Lethality is a critical concept that goes beyond the notion of looking at signs of abuse to really understanding the difference between an abusive relationship and a potentially lethally abusive relationship. All abusive relationships have the potential for lethality, but some have higher risks for it. Here I identify what enhances or increases the possibility of lethality. One of the main tools used to conduct lethality assessments is the Danger Assessment (Campbell, 1986, 2007; Snider, Webster, O'Sullivan, & Campbell, 2009). This tool (see pages 76–77) allows one to identify indicators of lethality. It does not suggest that lethality will be identified in every case or that this list is exhaustive. However, it provides a screening mechanism that highlights factors known to place women at significant risk for serious injury or death.

There are times when women meet men who have these identifiers and feel as though they can change the person. It is critical to realize that change is possible when the man takes responsibility for his behavior, evidences a commitment to change, and actively participates in getting the treatment needed to change the behavior. I often emphasize that a woman cannot change a man. The man must want to change himself. Therefore, when practitioners identify any of the indicators outlined in the Danger Assessment, it is imperative to remember that the perpetrator has made a choice to be violent and the survivor cannot change his choice. A previous history of abuse is an important indicator that should not be ignored, particularly if the person has been incarcerated for domestic violence or sexual assault or has had contact with law enforcement. Sometimes women ignore a man's previous history of violence and attribute his behavior to the other woman. History is the greatest indicator

DANGER ASSESSMENT

Jacquelyn C. Campbell, Ph.D., R.N.
Copyright 2003: www.dangerassessment.com

Several risk factors have been associated with increased risk of homicides (murders) of women and men in violent relationships. We cannot predict what will happen in your case, but we would like you to be aware of the danger of homicide in situations of abuse and for you to see how many of the risk factors apply to your situation.

Using the calendar, please mark the approximate dates during the past year when you were abused by your partner or ex-partner. Write on that date how bad the incident was according to the following scale:

1. Slapping, pushing; no injuries and/or continuing pain
2. Punching, kicking; bruises, cuts, and/or continuing pain
3. "Beating up"; severe contusions, burns, broken bones
4. Threat to use weapon; head injury, internal injury, permanent injury
5. Use of weapon; wounds from weapon

(If **any** of the descriptions for the higher number apply, use the higher number.)

Mark **Yes** or **No** for each of the following. ("He" refers to your husband, partner, ex-husband, ex-partner, or whoever is currently physically hurting you.)

____ 1. Has the physical violence increased in severity or frequency over the past year?

____ 2. Does he own a gun?

____ 3. Have you left him after living together during the past year?
      3a. (If have *never* lived with him, check ____)

____ 4. Is he unemployed?

____ 5. Has he ever used a weapon against you or threatened you with a lethal weapon?
          (If yes, was the weapon a gun?____)

____ 6. Does he threaten to kill you?

____ 7. Has he avoided being arrested for domestic violence?

____ 8. Do you have a child that is not his?

____ 9. Has he ever forced you to have sex when you did not wish to do so?

____ 10. Does he ever try to choke you?

____ 11. Does he use illegal drugs? By drugs, I mean "uppers" or amphetamines, "meth", speed, angel dust, cocaine, "crack", street drugs or mixtures.

____ 12. Is he an alcoholic or problem drinker?

____ 13. Does he control most or all of your daily activities? For instance: does he tell you who you can be friends with, when you can see your family, how much money you can use, or when you can take the car? (If he tries, but you do not let him, check here:____)

____14. Is he violently and constantly jealous of you? (For instance, does he say "if I can't have you, no one can.")

____ 15. Have you ever been beaten by him while you were pregnant? (If you have never been pregnant by him, check here:____)

____ 16. Has he ever threatened or tried to commit suicide?

____ 17. Does he threaten to harm your children?

____ 18. Do you believe he is capable of killing you?

____ 19. Does he follow or spy on you, leave threatening notes or messages, destroy your property, or call you when you don't want him to?

____ 20. Have you ever threatened or tried to commit suicide?

____ Total "Yes" Answers

Thank you. Please talk to your nurse, advocate or counselor about what the Danger Assessment means in terms of your situation.

of who he is and what he will be like in the relationship. The risk of violence increases by three when men relapse, and men are six times more severely violent toward an intimate partner when alcohol is involved (Klostermann, Kelley, Mignone, Pusateri, & Fals-Stewart, 2010). Women in a relationship with a man with an alcohol problem are more likely to be victimized by their partner (Dawson, Grant, Chou, & Stinson, 2007; Mcmurran & Gilchrist, 2008), so alcohol use should not be taken lightly. The risk for homicide by a perpetrator increases by seven when firearms are present in the home (Bailey, 1997), and more than one-half of murders of victims of domestic violence occur at the hand of a perpetrator with a gun. Consequently, firearms are a major risk factor that should be taken seriously. Thus, the Danger Assessment is a critical tool in assessing the risk of severe violence or death as a result of domestic violence.

What Can You Do?

In this section, I explore what practitioners and friends or community members can do to respond to domestic violence. How a practitioner responds to intimate partner violence is different from what is expected of a friend, family member, or member of the community. Practitioners must be guided by the NASW (2008) *Code of Ethics*. The NASW *Code of Ethics* provides guidelines on how to proceed, and although it may not contain specific language on how to address domestic violence, it provides a framework for how to help women with this issue. The *Code of Ethics* anchors social workers in an ethical code and professional discipline bigger than themselves. The *Code of Ethics* guides social workers' thinking in some specific ways, particularly in terms of self-determination, professional judgment, competent practice, informed consent, and use of supervision and consultation.

Self-Determination

Respect the woman's self-determination, meaning respect her right to make life decisions. I know this sounds ideological because the truth is that when a woman comes in and she is bruised and battered and the situation is becoming progressively worse, it gets harder and harder to be able to honor this key principle of the *Code of Ethics*. Yet self-determination speaks to the empowerment of the person. Creating opportunities for empowerment is important. People empower themselves. Competent practitioners facilitate the process of empowerment, so one thing that professionals have to focus on is creating opportunities for empowerment, understanding the dynamics and cycle of abuse. Opportunities can be created by providing literature, actively listening to the woman, not passing judgment, providing a safe space for her to keep personal records, or conducting safety planning with her at different times. So the notion of empowerment becomes important because it is not just an intangible process. Empowerment means that one is actually creating an opportunity for the woman to engage in action that reinforces her ability to address the relationship and the issues occurring in her life. It is about helping her to create opportunities for her to see the possibilities and move past the situation. It is also about recognizing her strength and resilience in responding to the situation in an effort to further support decisions that will ultimately lead to her safety and wellness. The practitioner has to believe and has to help the woman believe that her situation can change and then engage in the necessary actions to move toward that change.

Do Not Be Judgmental

Do not be judgmental. Practitioners may be frustrated with the situation and wonder why the survivor does not just leave it. The reality is that the practitioner may at times judge or blame the survivor for being in the situation. The *Code of Ethics* reminds practitioners that they are not in control of the client's process—the client is. The practitioner may be the only person in the survivor's life who can be nonjudgmental, so it is that much more important to provide support without judgment and create opportunities for the client to better understand her options. One of the major challenges for women is that they do not see their options or feel as though they have a lot of viable options. Therefore, the practitioner has a key opportunity to open the door to possible options and help the woman see the possibilities and how to access them in a safe manner. Consider this:

The woman may have not revealed the abuse to anyone outside of her inner circle. Therefore, the practitioner's reaction is that much more important. Being nonjudgmental helps to lessen the feelings of shame and self-blame that a woman seeking help for intimate partner violence often feels. It also gives the survivor a safe place to process and think through her choices. The ability to reserve judgment and instead use that energy to support the person will prove to be far more useful and effective in helping the survivor.

Competent Practice

Being competent in practicing in the area of intimate partner violence is critical. Practitioners must continuously seek opportunities for training in and learning about new assessment tools and interventions to assist clients. They must make an effort to become fully aware of the dynamics and challenges that survivors experience to be able to best assist the person. Survivors often reveal what they are experiencing in stages; therefore, assessments have to be ongoing. A practitioner can ask a woman whether she is experiencing violence during an intake session, and her answer will be no. However, six months later she may reveal that she is experiencing abuse. One reason for this is that the woman is trying to figure out how much she can share or risk sharing. Timing is key. She may be ashamed or not know that she is in a domestic violence situation. She may be in fear of her children being removed from the home as a result of the violence's being uncovered. Therefore, the professional must continuously assess the situation, ask questions, and look for signs of abuse. The professional must also develop a trusting relationship with the client that is built on her awareness of mandatory reporting requirements and the desire to be helpful and authentically supportive. Professionals must remember that although they are asking required questions, the woman provides them with some of the information along the way, and it requires ongoing assessment. Practitioners must also be careful about where they ask the questions and who is present when they ask them. Survivors will often not speak in front of the perpetrator or children, and practitioners can put the woman at risk for further violence by asking questions while the perpetrator or children are in the area. Doing this will also result in an altered and protected response anchored in the woman's survival strategies. Therefore, practitioners must strengthen their interpersonal, interviewing, listening, and questioning skills and their patience to optimize the assessment process. They cannot view their skill set as complete. They must have a continuous commitment to furthering their knowledge and skill in this changing area of practice.

Informed Consent, Privacy, and Confidentiality

Recognizing the responsibility to preserve confidentiality is critical. However, social workers must also be honest about the limitations of confidentiality. It is important that practitioners know the mandated reporting requirements. Social workers are required to report in three circumstances: (1) suspicion of child abuse or neglect, (2) suspicion that the person may hurt himself or herself, and (3) suspicion that the person may hurt another person.

Practitioners must ensure that the woman understands what constitutes a reason to break confidentiality. The risk is that the woman may not reveal information that could pose a safety risk and warrant a mandated report, but there is no way to prevent this from happening if she has made that choice. However, the ethical code requires that practitioners be honest about the limitations of confidentiality. Also, it is equally as, if not more, harmful to be dishonest or to withhold reporting requirements and then break confidentiality. Practitioners must be upfront with clients. You would be surprised how many survivors still share their stories despite the mandated reporting requirements. When the person is ready to be helped and has decided to make changes or is fearful for her life or the life of her family, she will forgo the lesser fear of mandated reporting and take the chance of revealing the abuse to get help.

Use of Supervision and Consultation

Supervision and consultation in this area are key. Through these mechanisms, the practitioner can gain greater self-awareness, learn new strategies and techniques, and better understand the dynamics of abuse being experienced by the survivor. It is important to explore both the feelings about and challenges of working with this population in supervision and consultation. Professionals must make a conscious effort to use supervision to improve working with the client and developing a greater awareness of the overall challenges being experienced in the client's life. Social work students continue to largely have limited awareness of the dynamics of domestic violence and how to effectively intervene with clients (Black, Weisz, & Bennett, 2010). Thus, the need for strong supervision and consultation is even more important in this area of practice.

Working with Family and Friends

Domestic violence has been identified as a major issue confronting the community. Community members, family, and friends are key resources to support finding solutions to domestic violence. I have found that family and friends often want to intervene but do not know how to address the problem. Here are some suggestions providers can share with family and friends.

- Do not assume that even though the person is a good friend she will tell you about the abuse. Do not be offended if she does not tell you. She may feel that you will judge her or look at her differently. She may be embarrassed. She may be afraid of your reaction to the perpetrator. It is important for you to not be upset but to instead spend your energy trying to support her and assuring her that you do not think less of her because of the situation.

- Friends often become frustrated with the survivor and the fact that she is still in the abusive relationship, which can become a real barrier to being helpful. Remember, survivors usually leave the relationship an average of eight times before they finally leave it for good. Expect her to go back and forth and know that it is part of the process.

- Accept the fact that some women just do not leave the relationship. This scenario can be tough for family and friends; however, continue to be supportive and share information and resources. Her not leaving the relationship does not mean she does not want change. It may mean she has not yet found the right solution.

- You can accompany her to court. If the court system is new to her, she will need your support and encouragement. The court system can be confusing, and an advocate may not be available to help survivors. In this situation, your encouragement will be that much more important. Your presence will remind her that she is not alone and that, in and of itself, is powerful.

- Share information with her. Share brochures, phone numbers, or Web sites that she can access to get help. If she is a friend or family member, do not counsel her yourself (even if you are a professional). Just point her in the right direction and create opportunities for professional dialogue and support. Recognize that the perpetrator could find this information and become upset. Therefore, think strategically with her about how and where to best access the information.

- Affirm her thinking and decision to be in a healthy relationship. She may be questioning herself and her decision making. By affirming her ability to make decisions, you are helping to strengthen her sense of self, which can lead to her empowerment and improved decision making. Encourage her to find someone who will respect and honor her. Remind her that she deserves to be in a healthy relationship. Let her know that a person who will love, honor, respect, and not violate her does exist. If she is unclear about what constitutes a healthy relationship, share that information with her.

- Do not take matters into your own hands. You may want to confront the perpetrator. In some situations, a confrontation is acceptable because of either your relationship with the perpetrator or your skill set, which allows you to understand how to best confront the person. If you lack the skill and understanding, you should not confront the person. Your threats could put the woman at even greater risk. Do not feel like you have failed if you have not confronted the perpetrator. You must remember that her safety and your safety are the priority, and the desire to show more power over the perpetrator is not helpful. This does not mean you cannot make it clear that you do not condone the violence, but you must first consider the safety of the survivor and family.

- You will want to resolve the problem your way, but you have to resist this urge. Recognize that even if you have experienced abuse, this situation is not your situation. People often want to solve the issue for the woman, but it is important that the woman work it through even if the result is staying in the relationship.

- Store sensitive information for her, such as bank records, immunization records, or birth certificates, or money that she has saved. This step is a part of safety planning, which is a key intervention. Ensure that you have a safe place for materials that she can access readily. You can be supportive, but do not try to come up with a safety plan yourself. Instead, have her talk with a professional who can help her develop a safety plan that will fit her unique needs. Safety planning is best done with the assistance and support of a professional. Leaving an abusive partner is a high-risk time period and should be done with professional assistance (Anderson & Saunders, 2003).

If She Chooses to Stay

The woman should

- develop a code word for the children and make sure they know where to go to be safe and how to access help

- make sure the people in her life know her situation

- practice how to get out of the residence safely

- make sure she has gas in the car or funds for transportation available

- contact the National Domestic Violence Hotline (1-800-799-SAFE [7233]) for a referral to a local service provider, safety tips, and other information about domestic violence

- back her car into the driveway so that it is facing in the direction of the street in case she has to leave quickly.

If She Chooses to Leave

The woman should

- remember that leaving the relationship can be the most dangerous time period in a domestic violence situation, so it is particularly important to conduct safety planning with a professional

- keep pictures of the abuse or any items that can prove what has taken place, such as bloody clothing or damaged items

- keep a journal; write down what is occurring so she has a record

- have a plan for where to go to get help; make sure that someone who can be trusted knows the plan; and make sure that she has both an emergency plan and a plan for nonemergency situations

- develop a code word for the children and make sure they know where to go to be safe and how to access help

- make sure the children have someone to contact if child removal becomes preeminent

- contact the National Domestic Violence Hotline (1-800-799-SAFE [7233]) for a referral to a local service provider, safety tips, and other information about domestic violence

- maintain her documents and critical papers and have quick access to money so that she can make a move

- maintain records of the abuse, including police reports, protection orders, and emergency room or doctor's visits.

Important Items to Keep at All Times

These items should be stored in a secured and accessible location, such as church, with a family member or friend, or with the social worker.

- spare car keys
- driver's license

- immigration papers
- credit card numbers
- insurance information
- children's immunization records
- medication and prescription information
- money
- phone numbers for vital people and organizations
- copies of birth certificates and health records
- legal documents and protection orders

Reflecting Pool

In this chapter, I wrote about the signs of abuse and lethality indicators. I also outlined how practitioners and community members, family, or friends can be more responsive to intimate partner violence. Now consider how you have responded to intimate partner violence in the past and what has affected your response. In the Reflecting Pool, I challenge you to think about how you have responded to domestic violence and how you can improve or strengthen your response.

My Reflection

One day while at home, I heard a man screaming loudly. I quickly looked out my window and saw the man with a woman. He screamed at her and berated her. Then he grabbed her by the arms and continued to scream at her. My mind began to race. "What should I do? If I call the police, he might think someone from my house called it in and then my family could be in danger. If I go outside and try to help her, I could end up getting hurt as well." I made a loud noise so that he knew someone was watching. Then, I called the police. By the time I returned to the window, they were both gone. Many people have been in a situation where they have witnessed abuse. It is important to consider how to maintain your safety while still being responsive. I hope that by recognizing the signs of abuse, understanding lethality indicators, and knowing more about what they can do, practitioners can be more responsive to intimate partner violence. Maintain your safety at all times.

Your Reflection

- How do you think you can better respond to domestic violence?
- What can you do the next time the issue presents itself?
- What do you need to learn to be more effective in responding to this issue?
- What has affected your response to domestic violence?
- If you have been exposed to intimate partner violence, how has that exposure shaped your response?

Notes:

_____

_____

_____

_____

_____

_____

_____

_____

_____

_____

_____

_____

_____

_____

_____

_____

_____

_____

References

Anderson, D., & Saunders, D. (2003). Leaving an abusive partner. *Trauma, Violence & Abuse, 4,* 163–191.

Bailey, J. E. (1997). Risk factors for violent death of women in the home. *Archives of Internal Medicine, 157,* 777–782.

Black, B., Weisz, A., & Bennett, L. (2010). Graduating social work students' perspectives on domestic violence. *Affilia: Journal of Women and Social Work, 25,* 173–184.

Campbell, J. (1986). Nursing assessment for the risk of homicide with battered women. *Advances in Nursing Science, 8,* 36–51.

Campbell, J. (2007). *Assessing dangerousness: Violence by batterers and child abusers* (2nd ed.). New York: Springer.

Dawson, D., Grant, B., Chou, S. P., & Stinson, F. (2007). The impact of partner alcohol problems on women's physical and mental health. *Journal of Studies on Alcohol & Drugs, 68,* 66–75.

Klostermann, K., Kelley, M. L., Mignone, T., Pusateri, L., & Fals-Stewart, W. (2010). Partner violence and substance abuse: Treatment interventions. *Aggression and Violent Behavior, 15,* 162–166.

Mcmurran, M., & Gilchrist, E. (2008). Anger control and alcohol use: Appropriate interventions for perpetrators of domestic violence? *Psychology, Crime and Law, 14,* 107–116.

National Association of Social Workers. (2008). *Code of ethics of the National Association of Social Workers.* Washington, DC: Author.

Snider, C., Webster, D., O'Sullivan, C., & Campbell, J. (2009). Intimate partner violence: Development of a brief risk assessment for the emergency department. *Academic Emergency Medicine, 16,* 1208–1216.

Select Resources

- *American Bar Association:* http://new.abanet.org/domesticviolence/Pages/default.aspx

- *Danger Assessment:* http://www.dangerassessment.org/WebApplication1/

- *House of Ruth:* http://www.hruth.org/

- *National Domestic Violence Fatality Review Initiative:* http://www.ndvfri.org

- *National Domestic Violence Hotline:* http://www.thehotline.org/

- *National Network to End Domestic Violence:* http://www.nnedv.org/

- *National Women's Health Information Center:* http://www.womenshealth.gov/violence/state/

- *Safe Horizon:* http://www.safehorizon.org/

Five

Intimate Partner Violence Touches Every Area of the Heart

The next question I often hear is "Why should I care?" The person may not know someone who has experienced or witnessed abuse. Although the issue itself should warrant a desire to address the problem, for some people that is not enough. To these people, I respond by saying, "Because intimate partner violence connects with the issue you do care about." The unfortunate reality is that intimate partner violence is often connected to many of the issues that people care most about. That fact speaks to the pervasiveness and magnitude of the problem. I believe that as people begin to better understand how intimate partner violence connects to issues that they care about, they will be more committed to addressing it. In this chapter, I show how intimate partner violence connects with several major social issues. Specifically, I focus on the intersection between intimate partner violence and substance abuse, child welfare, health, mental health, prisoner reentry, and disaster planning.

Substance Abuse and Intimate Partner Violence

Substance abuse and intimate partner violence are significantly linked. As discussed earlier in the book, substance abuse does not cause intimate partner violence; however, the connection between these two issues is undeniable. More than one-half of couples with substance abuse problems experience intimate partner violence (Klostermann, Kelley, Mignone, Pusateri, & Fals-Stewart, 2010). One study found that alcohol or drugs were involved in at least one-third of domestic violence cases in state courts, with alcohol being used most often (Smith & Farole, 2009). Most offenders who have killed or attempted to kill an intimate partner were under the influence of a substance (Sharps, Campbell, Campbell, Gary, & Webster, 2003). The risk for more serious and lethal violence is compounded by substance abuse, particularly by alcohol use (Caetano, Schafer, & Cunradi, 2001; Poole, Greaves, Jategaonkar, McCullough, & Chabot, 2008). One-half of men in batterers intervention groups have substance abuse problems, and one-half of men in substance abuse programs are perpetrators of intimate partner violence (Thomas & Bennett, 2009). Survivors with substance-abusing partners are often more likely to be victimized than those with non-substance-abusing partners (Dawson, Grant, Chou, & Stinson, 2007). They are also more likely to experience problems with mental health, injury, increased stress, and a poorer quality of life (Dawson et al., 2007). Researchers are still developing an understanding of how prescription drug use is connected to intimate partner violence. Both batterers intervention program directors and domestic violence shelter directors have acknowledged that substance abuse must be addressed and better integrated into service delivery and treatment (Dalton, 2009; Fowler, 2009; Thomas & Bennett, 2009).

Survivors often use substances to self-medicate and mask the pain of being in an abusive relationship. The ability to function is significantly diminished when substance abuse is involved (Lee, Ju, & Lightfoot, 2010). When survivors receive treatment in a safe space, substance abuse decreases (Poole et al., 2008). The need to provide and expand services to women who are both substance abusers and survivors of domestic violence is critical.

Child Welfare Connection

Child welfare and domestic violence are intricately connected (Antle, Barbee, Yankeelov, & Bledsoe, 2010; Humphreys, 2007a; Hoyle, 2008; O. Williams, Griffin, Davis, & Bennett, 2006). Domestic violence, family violence, and child maltreatment have been estimated to co-occur in 30 to 60 percent of cases (Chipungu & Bent-Goodley, 2004; Little & Kaufman Kantor, 2002). More than 15 million children are witnesses to intimate partner violence each year (Whitfield, Anda, Dube, & Felittle, 2003). Each day, more than 16,000 children reside in domestic violence shelters with their mother to stay safe from abuse (National Network to End Domestic Violence, 2009). Analyzing the National Survey of Child and Adolescent Well-Being, Kohl, Barth, Hazen, and Landsverk (2005) found that 12 percent of child welfare caseworkers identified the co-occurrence of domestic violence with child welfare, and close to one-third of the caregivers reported experiencing domestic violence.

In some cases, the primary reason the case was referred to the child welfare system is intimate partner violence; in other cases, the violence is revealed over time. Schools may also become involved if child protective services is called because of educational neglect. Many children stay home from school to protect their mother from the abuser or to assure themselves that nothing will happen to their mother. The educational neglect gets the family into the child welfare system, but the domestic violence is at the center of the issue. Mothers in the child protective services system often do not reveal the abuse for several reasons: distrust of child welfare workers, the belief that the worker will immediately remove the child on hearing about the domestic violence, and the perception that the worker will look down on them for being in an abusive relationship (Mandel, 2010).

Child welfare professionals and domestic violence advocates continue to debate how best to respond to child protection issues when domestic violence is uncovered. Domestic violence advocates believe that mothers are often revictimized by the child welfare system, particularly when the child is removed immediately because of the perception that domestic violence is a form of child abuse or neglect. They also state that many mothers are motivated to leave the relationship when they see that the children are at risk of being removed from the home because of their commitment and desire to protect the children. Child welfare workers reinforce that their focus is on providing a safe environment for the child and that the mother is not the primary client. They also emphasize that some mothers do not protect the child from the abuse and that children can be hurt in situations in which they attempt to protect the survivor or when the survivor uses the child to protect herself. Concerns have been expressed for the disproportionate focus on women's responsibility to protect, leave, or force the perpetrator to leave as opposed to holding the perpetrator accountable for the abuse (Devaney, 2009; Douglas & Walsh, 2010; Guille, 2004; Hartley, 2004; Lapierre, 2008). That mothers actively use strategies to physically protect their children is increasingly being recognized; however, protecting the children emotionally and psychologically presents greater difficulty (Haight, Shim, Linn, & Swinford, 2007). It has been suggested that greater effort be placed on creating a perpetrator risk assessment in child welfare that will hold the perpetrator accountable and reinforce the importance of the father's responsibility in the child welfare process (Crooks, Goodall, Baker, & Hughes, 2006). A call has gone out to ensure that the perpetrator does not use kinship care as a tool to further control and manipulate the survivor through the knowing or unknowing cooperation of family members brought into the situation after child removal (Bent-Goodley & Brade, 2007).

The child welfare system has been called on to develop a broader understanding of what child protection looks like when domestic violence is present (Antle et al., 2010; Humphreys, 2008; Rivett & Kelly, 2006). Researchers have discussed the notion that both areas must come together to serve women and children (Magen, Conroy, & Del Tufo, 2000; Moles, 2008). For example, when domestic violence is identified, the rate of child maltreatment is higher and more severe largely because of the isolation associated with domestic violence and a more limited social support system (Becky et al., 2007; Kohl, Edleson, English, & Barth, 2005). Yet despite this, domestic violence is still not viewed as a major contributing factor in the child welfare decision-making process (Postmus & Ortega, 2005; Saunders & Anderson, 2000). The policies and protocols guiding this area of practice continue to be limited (Fairtlough, 2006). The application of standardized criteria for assessment and intervention is needed, as is awareness of how cumulative risks increase child welfare decision making and ongoing training in this area (Button & Payne, 2009; Coohey, 2007; Kohl & Macy, 2008). Child welfare workers are called on to understand the impact of exposure to intimate partner violence on children. Exposure to domestic violence, even as early as infancy and toddlerhood, can result in posttraumatic stress disorder (PTSD) (Lieberman, 2007). Older children may experience other symptoms as a result of witnessing domestic violence, such as truancy, withdrawal from friends, hypervigilance, aggression, or anxiety. Family and child functioning improves through early intervention, crisis intervention, building family supports and community partnerships, cross-disciplinary strategies, and coordinated care that addresses the family's multiple needs (Hyde, Lamb, Arteaga, & Chavis, 2008). Key to providing these services are strong assessment tools and protocols that identify the risks associated with both domestic violence and child welfare and ongoing training to address how to use the tools and how perceptions of domestic violence affect practice (Button & Payne, 2009; Coohey, 2007; Darlington, Healy, & Feeney, 2010; Shlonsky & Friend, 2007; K. Williams & Grant, 2006). These assessments need to extend beyond the woman to include perpetrator risk assessments that hold men accountable and assess the impact the perpetrator has on the home environment and the children (Crooks et al., 2006; Humphreys, 2007b).

Impact on Children of Witnessing Domestic Violence

- *Psychological:* depression, low self-esteem, trauma-related symptoms, anxiety disorders, helplessness, guilt, rage, flashbacks, intrusive thoughts, shame, betrayal, volatile behavior

- *Physical:* headache, stomachache, sleep disorders, nightmares, use of alcohol or drugs, low infant birthweight, disability, bed wetting

- *Social:* poor social skills, aggression, inability to make or keep friends, poor school performance, sudden change in friends or behavior, truancy, overachievement, running away from home

Remember that these behaviors can be different on the basis of the child's age and development.

Health and Intimate Partner Violence

The connection between health and intimate partner violence is another critical area. Women are more likely to suffer from chronic disease as a result of domestic violence, for example, hypertension, heart conditions, emphysema, diabetes, kidney and liver disease, headaches, gastrointestinal problems, abdominal pain, pelvic pain, sleep disorders, arthritis, chronic neck and back pain, and ulcers (Campbell et al., 2002; Coker, Smith, Bethea, King, & McKeown, 2000; Humphreys, Lowe, & Williams, 2009). These chronic problems result in domestic violence survivors' being 80 percent more likely to have a stroke, 70 percent more likely to have heart disease, 60 percent more likely to have asthma, and 70 percent more likely to have an alcohol problem (Centers for Disease Control and Prevention, 2008). The connections between domestic violence and pregnancy, traumatic brain injury (TBI), oral health, and HIV have received increased attention.

Pregnancy and Intimate Partner Violence

Pregnancy is a particularly high-risk time period in a woman's life. Fifteen percent of pregnant women have reported at least one episode of violence during pregnancy (Datner, Wiebe, Brensinger, & Nelson, 2007). More than 300,000 pregnant women have been estimated to experience some form of abuse during pregnancy resulting in serious pregnancy complications, such as miscarriage, low weight gain, infections, and bleeding (Parker, McFarlane, & Soeken, 1994). Almost one-third of maternal injury-related deaths occur from a pregnant mother's being killed by a perpetrator (Chang, Berg, Saltzman, & Herndon, 2005). Consequently, the practitioner must remain particularly vigilant during this time period. The man could be jealous of the attention being given to the pregnant woman or the baby in utero. At the same time, the woman could have more needs and require more support during the pregnancy. She could be more dependent on her partner, particularly in a high-risk pregnancy. All of these dynamics are critical to address.

Traumatic Brain Injury (TBI) and Intimate Partner Violence

TBI is also linked to domestic violence. One study found that three-quarters of survivors had experienced at least one brain injury and one-half had multiple brain injuries resulting from domestic violence (Valera & Berenbaum, 2003). Between 40 percent and 50 percent of women in domestic violence relationships have lost consciousness during a battering incident (Banks, 2007; Jackson, Philp, Nuttall, & Diller, 2002). These injuries are often a result of blows to the head, being hit in the face, or being severely shaken during an abusive incident. The short-term effects of TBI include dizziness, headaches, nausea, and loss of consciousness. Long-term consequences include trouble concentrating, memory loss, difficulty focusing, lack of cognitive flexibility, learning challenges, anxiety, PTSD, general distress, depression, neurological injuries, facial injuries, seizures, and permanent disability (Banks, 2007; Valera & Berenbaum, 2003). It is imperative that health providers be aware of these links, conduct assessments without the perpetrator being present, and include domestic violence in screening for those with TBI. Providers must also be aware of the impact of TBI on the woman's cognitive functioning, emotional and mental well-being, and decision making.

Oral Health and Intimate Partner Violence

The link between domestic violence and oral health is also critical. Dental providers often treat women for injuries inflicted by an abusive partner. Most domestic violence injuries can be found in the region of the head, neck, and mouth (Danley, Gansky, Chow, & Gerbert, 2004; Nelms, Gutmann, Solomon, Dewald, & Campbell, 2008). The woman may have injuries to the teeth, soft tissue, and jaw; neglected oral hygiene; and difficulty eating because of the injuries. Most dental providers do not screen for domestic violence, and even when injuries are present, they do not ask about them (Nelms et al., 2008). Increasingly, domestic violence screening, assessment, referral, and the role of dental providers are being included in dental education (Danley et al., 2004; KwonHsieh, Herzig, Gansky, Danley, & Gerbert, 2006). Because so many women experience injuries in these areas, it is imperative that oral providers do the appropriate screening for domestic violence and be prepared to make referrals. Building relationships with local domestic violence providers and having domestic violence–related information in the offices of dental providers should be a standard practice.

HIV and Intimate Partner Violence

The connection between domestic violence and HIV has been well established (Josephs & Abel, 2009; Lichtenstein, 2006; Teitelman, Ratcliffe, Morales-Aleman, & Sullivan, 2008; Wyatt, Axelrod, Chin, Vargas Carmona, & Burns Loeb, 2000). Women often do not fully grasp the risks associated with domestic violence and its intersection with HIV/AIDS (Cole, Logan, & Shannon, 2008). Even domestic violence shelters are trying to create more collaborative supports for women at the intersection of these issues, recognizing the grave risks associated with them (Rountree, Pomeroy, & Marsiglia, 2008).

HIV/AIDS is connected to domestic violence in many ways (Bent-Goodley, 2007; El-Bassel, Caldeira, Ruglass, & Gilbert, 2009; Frye et al., 2007; Josephs & Abel, 2009; Pinkham & Malinowska-Sempruch, 2008; Teitelman et al., 2008; Wingood & DiClemente, 1997):

- transaction or exchange sex, in which sex is forced by an intimate partner in exchange for money, materials, or other items
- high-risk sexual behaviors, such as forced anal or oral sex
- the inability to negotiate condom usage because of the threat of violence
- forced sex with a partner who is unfaithful or with multiple partners
- being forced to engage in unwanted sex
- violence that can result from revealing one's HIV status
- being denied access to HIV services and medication adherence because of domestic violence

Risks for HIV and domestic violence are increased because of the woman's inability to access care, high rates of sexual abuse, discrimination in health care, low socioeconomic status, having sex at an early age, infidelity in the relationship, girls having sex with an older partner, and drug use (Arriaga, 2002; Cole et al., 2008; Kalicharan, Williams, Cherry, Belchar, & Nachimson, 1998; Lichtenstein, 2006; Mitchell Fuentes, 2008; Witte, El-Bassel, Gilbert, Wu, & Chang, 2010; Young, Washington, Jerman, & Tak, 2007). The connection between domestic violence and HIV must be considered and examined, particularly in relation to developing culturally appropriate responses to the diversity of risks for different populations of women. By addressing the intersection of HIV and domestic violence, practitioners are better able to serve and support clients and can help them better understand impending risk factors.

Health Care Response to Intimate Partner Violence

Many women use the health care system as a result of intimate partner violence. More than 5 million women annually access care seeking treatment for issues of intimate partner violence. The health care system spends more than $8 billion per year on the mental and physical impacts of domestic violence (Max, Rice, Finkelstein, Bardwell, & Leadbetter, 2004). Despite this, fewer than one-fifth of survivors seeking medical treatment for intimate partner violence–related injuries are identified by health providers (Bureau of Justice Statistics, 2006). The health system is continually examining assessment and screening tools to ensure that domestic violence is better detected and that greater resources and referrals are available to address the problem. Domestic violence screening protocols are critical and have been developed to identify domestic violence within health care settings (Hamberger & Phelan, 2006; Klap, Tang, Wells, Starks, & Rodriguez, 2007; Thurston, Tutty, Eisener, Lalonde, Belenky, & Osborne, 2009). In addition to screening for domestic violence, health care settings have been called on to begin educational initiatives, develop protocol and policy, and increase environmental cues such as brochures and posters to encourage dialogue, awareness, and access to information (Hamberger & Phelan, 2006). These health issues are exacerbated among women of color because of disparities in health care resulting from unequal access to care, discrimination in care, poorer quality of care, and lack of cultural proficiency on behalf of health care providers and systems (Bent-Goodley, 2007; Humphreys, 2007b).

Mental Health and Intimate Partner Violence

The connection between domestic violence and mental health is also clear (Goodwin, Chandler, & Meisel, 2003; Mourad, Levendosky, Bogat, & Eye, 2008). Survivors are three times more likely to be depressed and two times more likely to suffer from anxiety; nearly 40 percent have considered suicide. Between 17 percent and 72 percent suffer from depression; 33 percent to 88 percent, PTSD; and 33 percent, anxiety disorders (Goodwin et al., 2003; Warshaw & Barnes, 2003). Higher levels of psychological abuse are linked to greater poor health-related outcomes and chronic disease (Coker et al., 2000). Clearly, intimate partner violence increases the risk for experiencing mental health challenges. However, having a mental health issue can also place a woman at risk for experiencing intimate partner violence. Among a group of women with psychiatric disorders assessed for domestic violence, 30 percent to 60 percent had experienced domestic violence (Howard et al., 2010). Despite this risk, treatment plans did not include a focus on domestic violence assessment or referrals. Women often experience multiple emotional problems that are further evidenced through the identification of PTSD (Johansen, Wahl, Eilertsen, & Weisaeth, 2007). These emotional issues can have long-term consequences for mental health, stability in relationships and living situations, and employment that go beyond the abusive incident (Krause, Kaltman, Goodman, & Dutton, 2008). Too many mental health providers still do not understand the dynamics and cycle of domestic violence and consequently provide little to no treatment for the abuse. Rather than addressing just the symptomatology, efforts must be made to address the mental health issues within the context of the domestic violence being experienced or previously experienced.

Disasters and Intimate Partner Violence

Disasters also have a serious impact on and are affected by domestic violence. After a disaster, more survivors experience severe injuries and increased lethality as a result of domestic violence (Chew & Ramdas, 2005; Gault, Hartmann, Jones-DeWeever, Werschkul, & Williams, 2005). For example, sexual abuse increased by 20 percent and domestic violence by 80 percent after Hurricane Katrina. Issues of gender-based violence overall rose from 4.6 per 100,000 per day to 16.3 per 100,000 per day (nearly four times higher; Anastario, Shehab, & Lawry, 2009). Services are particularly strained after disasters. The environment is often chaotic, facilities are overcrowded, and lawlessness often reigns because of lessened or a lack of police protection. These issues are exacerbated by existing inequity and social vulnerabilities experienced by women and particularly by poor women and women of color (Enarson, 1999; Fisher, 2010; Jenkins & Phillips, 2008; Jones-DeWeever, 2006; Wraith, 1997). Consequently, the gender-based vulnerabilities that women experience after a disaster must be examined as they connect to predisaster social, economic, and political conditions for women (Pyles & Lewis, 2007; Reese, 2004; Tanskanen et al., 2004). Because of the profession's commitment to social and economic justice, social workers must be particularly committed to being involved in responding to disasters, particularly as social work relates to the unique needs of women, poor women, women with disabilities, and women with language barriers.

Prisoner Reentry and Intimate Partner Violence

More than 600,000 formerly incarcerated people return home to their communities annually. The transition back to the community and family is the target of discussion in many local communities (Visher, Kachnowski,

LaVigne, & Travis, 2004; Visher, LaVigne, & Travis, 2004). Prisoner reentry is another important issue that intersects with intimate partner violence. Parole system policies and procedures to address the issue of intimate partner violence are receiving increased attention. Intimate partner violence can continue while a man is incarcerated. The man can use family and community networks and phone calls from prison to further abuse a survivor despite not being physically present. The perpetrator's ability to control the survivor from within prison walls can continue after his release, particularly because parole and domestic violence systems remain disconnected. It is important to understand that abuse can continue even when the perpetrator is incarcerated. Issues identified by survivors in this population include

- the stressors placed on the woman while the man is incarcerated and when he transitions home
- the impact of prison culture on the man and the challenges placed on the relationship as a result
- the increased vulnerability of the woman in the relationship related to intimate partner abuse and HIV infection
- the lack of clarity of roles and mistrust in criminal justice systems (Oliver & Hairston, 2006)

The next issue is that when the incarcerated person is released or wants to be released, the woman should be notified. It is critical that parole officers meet with the woman during the prerelease phase, in the time leading up to the release, and after the release to determine an appropriate place for the man to go and to identify safety considerations for the woman and children. The woman's capacity to be truthful when asked about the man's release and conditions may be affected due to abuse. With HIV proliferating in prisons, consideration needs to be given to aid for women that integrates intimate partner violence and HIV services. An additional consideration is whether the man has received batterers intervention services while incarcerated. The connection between prisoner reentry and domestic violence as it relates to domestic violence must be better addressed. Systems and protocols must be developed to better address how women are placed at risk both during the man's incarceration and after his release back into the community.

Reflecting Pool

Understanding that intimate partner violence connects with other major social issues is key to developing responses that go beyond a particular group. This acknowledgment also allows practitioners to develop more integrated responses that recognize that many of their clients are juggling multiple issues and so systems must better accommodate responses that will meet their needs.

My Reflection

I was preparing to engage faith-based groups in a project to educate churches about domestic violence prevention. Many people asked me why I wanted to work with churches, the perception being that churches did not want to address this issue. I began my relationship building by talking about the local statistics related to intimate partner violence in the area. This information included a focus on the number of women whose lives had been lost because of intimate partner violence within the local community. I also included information about each denomination's national policies on domestic violence and how the project could help them meet their denomination's expectations in this area. Sadly, each time I found a lack of interest and willingness to open up the church to exploring this topic. However, I noticed that the churches had prison ministries; substance ministries; and health, marriage, and singles ministries. I also noticed that they had youth ministries, women's ministries, men's ministries, and even HIV ministries. After reviewing what was important to the church, I began to talk about how intimate partner violence connected with the issues most important to the church. No matter the issue, I could talk about the church's important role in responding to issues they cared about and those issues' intersection with domestic violence. In the end, all of the churches agreed to partner with me on the project—not initially because of their commitment to intimate partner violence but instead because of their commitment to an issue that was important to them and my ability to connect it with intimate partner violence. Practitioners have to help others understand these connections and why it matters to them to address this issue.

Your Reflection

- What are the issues most important to you, and how does intimate partner violence intersect with them?

- How would you respond if the focus was on an area or group related to intimate partner violence that mattered to you?

- How can you better connect with others on the basis of their issue and intimate partner violence?

- What is your understanding of how intimate partner violence connects with other issues?

Notes:

_____

_____

_____

_____

_____

_____

_____

_____

_____

_____

References

Anastario, M., Shehab, N., & Lawry, L. (2009). Increased gender-based violence among women internally displaced in Mississippi 2 years post-Hurricane Katrina. _Disaster Medicine and Public Health Preparedness, 3,_ 18–26.

Antle, B., Barbee, A., Yankeelov, P., & Bledsoe, L. (2010). A qualitative evaluation of the effects of mandatory reporting of domestic violence on victims and their children. _Journal of Family Social Work, 13,_ 56–73.

Arriaga, A. (2002). HIV/AIDS and violence against women. *Human Rights, 29,* 18.

Banks, M. (2007). Overlooked but critical: Traumatic brain injury as a consequence of interpersonal violence. *Trauma, Violence & Abuse, 8,* 290–298.

Becky, F. A., Barbee, A., Sullivan, D., Yankeelov, P., Johnson, L., & Cunningham, M. (2007). The relationship between domestic violence and child neglect. *Brief Treatment and Crisis Intervention, 7,* 364–382.

Bent-Goodley, T. B. (2007). Health disparities and violence against women: Why and how cultural and societal influences matter. *Trauma, Violence, & Abuse, 8,* 90–104.

Bent-Goodley, T. B., & Brade, K. (2007). Domestic violence and kinship care. *Journal of Health and Social Policy, 22,* 65–84.

Bureau of Justice Statistics. (2006). *Intimate partner violence in the United States.* Washington, DC: Author.

Button, D., & Payne, B. (2009). Training child protective services workers about domestic violence: Needs, strategies and barriers. *Children and Youth Services Review, 31,* 364–369.

Caetano, R., Schafer, J., & Cunradi, C. (2001). Alcohol-related intimate partner violence among white, black and Hispanic couples in the United States. *Alcohol Research & Health, 25,* 58–65.

Campbell, J., Jones, A., Dienemann, J., Kub, J., Schollenberger, J., O'Campo, P., et al. (2002). Intimate partner violence and physical health consequences. *Archives of Internal Medicine, 162,* 1157–1164.

Centers for Disease Control and Prevention. (2008). *Adverse health conditions and health risk behaviors associated with intimate partner violence. Morbidity and Mortality Weekly Report, 57,* 113–117.

Chang, J., Berg, C., Saltzman, L., & Herndon, J. (2005). Homicide: A leading cause of injury deaths among pregnant and postpartum women in the United States 1991–1999. *American Journal of Public Health, 95,* 471–477.

Chew, L., & Ramdas, K. (2005). *Caught in the storm: The impact of natural disasters on women.* San Francisco: Global Fund for Women.

Chipungu, S. S., & Bent-Goodley, T. B. (2004). Challenges of contemporary foster care: Ensuring safe, stable, and supportive homes for children. *Future of Children, 14,* 75–94.

Coker, A. L., Davis, K. E., Arias, I., Desai, S., Sanderson, M., Brandt, H. M., & Smith, P. H. (2002). Physical and mental health effects of intimate partner violence for men and women. *American Journal of Preventive Medicine, 23,* 260–268.

Coker, A., Smith, P., Bethea, L., King, M., & McKeown, R. (2000). Physical health consequences of physical and psychological intimate partner violence. *Archives of Medicine, 9,* 451–457.

Cole, J., Logan, T. K., & Shannon, L. (2008). Self-perceived risk of HIV among women with protective orders against male partners. *Health & Social Work, 33,* 287–298.

Coohey, C. (2007). What criteria do child protective services investigators use to substantiate exposure to domestic violence? *Child Welfare, 86,* 93–122.

Crooks, C., Goodall, G., Baker, L., & Hughes, R. (2006). Preventing violence against women: Engaging the fathers of today and tomorrow. *Cognitive and Behavioral Practice, 13,* 82–93.

Dalton, B. (2009). Battered program directors' view on substance abuse and domestic violence. *Journal of Aggression, Maltreatment & Trauma, 18,* 248–260.

Danley, D., Gansky, S. A., Chow, D., & Gerbert, B. (2004). Preparing dental students to recognize and respond to domestic violence. *Journal of the American Dental Association, 135,* 67–73.

Darlington, Y., Healy, K., & Feeney, J. (2010). Approaches to assessment and intervention across four types of child and family welfare services. *Children and Youth Services Review, 32,* 356–364.

Datner, E., Wiebe, D., Brensinger, C., & Nelson, D. (2007). Identifying pregnant women experiencing domestic violence in an urban emergency department. *Journal of Interpersonal Violence, 22,* 124–135.

Dawson, D., Grant, B., Chou, S. P., & Stinson, F. (2007). The impact of partner alcohol problems on women's physical and mental health. *Journal of Studies on Alcohol & Drugs, 68,* 66–75.

Devaney, J. (2009). Children's exposure to domestic violence: Holding men to account. *Political Quarterly, 80,* 569–574.

Douglas, H., & Walsh, T. (2010). Mothers, domestic violence, and child protection. *Violence Against Women, 16,* 489–508.

El-Bassel, N., Caldeira, N. A., Ruglass, L. M., & Gilbert, L. (2009). Addressing the unique needs of African American women in HIV prevention. *American Journal of Public Health, 99,* 996–1001.

Enarson, E. (1999). Violence against women in disasters: A study of domestic violence programs in the United States and Canada. *Violence Against Women, 5,* 742–768.

Fairtlough, A. (2006). Social work with children affected by domestic violence: An analysis of policy and practice implications. *Journal of Emotional Abuse, 6,* 25–47.

Fisher, S. (2010). Violence against women and natural disasters: Findings from post-tsunami Sri Lanka. *Violence Against Women, 16,* 902–918.

Fowler, D. (2009). Screening for co-occurring intimate partner abuse and substance abuse: Challenges across service delivery system. *Journal of Social Work Practice in the Addictions, 9,* 318–339.

Frye, V., Latka, M. H., Yingfeng, W., Valverde, E. E., Knowlton, A. R., Knight, K. R., & O'Leary, A. (2007). Intimate partner violence perpetration against main female partners among HIV-positive male injection drug users. *JAIDS: Journal of Acquired Immune Deficiency Syndromes, 46,* 101–109.

Gault, B., Hartmann, H., Jones-DeWeever, A., Werschkul, M., & Williams, E. (2005). *The women of New Orleans and the Gulf Coast: Multiple disadvantages and key assets for recovery. Part I: Poverty, race, gender and class.* Washington, DC: Institute for Women's Policy Research.

Goodwin, S., Chandler, D., & Meisel, J. (2003). *Violence against women: The role of welfare reform.* Washington, DC: National Institute of Justice.

Guille, L. (2004). Men who batter and their children: An integrated review. *Aggression and Violent Behavior, 9,* 129–163.

Haight, W., Shim, W., Linn, L., & Swinford, L. (2007). Mothers' strategies for protecting children from batterers: The perspectives of battered women involved in child protective services. *Child Welfare, 86,* 41–62.

Hamberger, L. K., & Phelan, M. (2006). Domestic violence screening in medical and mental health care settings: Overcoming barriers to screening, identifying, and helping partner violence victims. *Journal of Aggression, Maltreatment & Trauma, 13,* 61–99.

Hartley, C. (2004). Severe domestic violence and child maltreatment: Considering child physical abuse, neglect, and failure to protect. *Children and Youth Services Review, 26,* 373–392.

Howard, L., Trevillion, K., Khalifeh, H., Woodall, A., Agnew-Davies, R., & Feder, G. (2010). Domestic violence and severe psychiatric disorders: Prevalence and interventions. *Psychological Medicine, 40,* 881–893.

Hoyle, C. (2008). Will she be safe? A critical analysis of risk assessment in domestic violence cases. *Children & Youth Services Review, 30,* 323–337.

Humphreys, C. (2007a). Domestic violence and child protection: Exploring the role of perpetrator risk assessments. *Child & Family Social Work, 12,* 360–369.

Humphreys, C. (2007b). A health inequalities perspective on violence against women. *Health and Social Care in the Community, 15,* 120–127.

Humphreys, C. (2008). Problems in the system of mandatory reporting of children living with domestic violence. *Journal of Family Studies, 14,* 228–239.

Humphreys, C., Lowe, P., & Williams, S. (2009). Sleep disruption and domestic violence: Exploring the interconnections between mothers and children. *Child & Family Social Work, 14,* 6–14.

Hyde, M., Lamb, Y., Arteaga, S., & Chavis, D. (2008). National evaluation of the Safe Start demonstration project: Implications for mental health practice. *Best Practice in Mental Health: An International Journal, 4,* 108–122.

Jackson, H., Philp, E., Nuttall, R., & Diller, L. (2002). Traumatic brain injury: A hidden consequence for battered women. *Professional Psychology: Research and Practice, 33,* 39–45.

Jenkins, P., & Phillips, B. (2008). Battered women, catastrophe, and the context of safety after Hurricane Katrina. *NWSA Journal, 20,* 49–68.

Johansen, V., Wahl, A. Eilertsen, D., & Weisaeth, L. (2007). Prevalence and predictors of post-traumatic stress disorder (PTSD) in physically injured victims of non-domestic violence. *Social Psychiatry & Psychiatric Epidemiology, 42,* 583–593.

Jones-DeWeever, A. (2006). *Women in the wake of the storm: Examining the post-Katrina realities of the women of New Orleans and the Gulf Coast.* Washington, DC: Institute for Women's Policy Research.

Josephs, L., & Abel, E. (2009). Investigating the relationship between intimate partner violence and HIV risk-propensity in black/African-American women. *Journal of Family Violence, 24,* 221–229.

Kalicharan, S. C., Williams, E. A., Cherry, C., Belcher, L., & Nachimson, D. (1998). Sexual coercion, domestic violence, and negotiating condom use among low-income African American women. *Journal of Women's Health, 7,* 371–378.

Klap, R., Tang, L., Wells, K., Starks, S., & Rodriguez, M. (2007). Screening for domestic violence among adult women in the United States. *Journal of General Internal Medicine, 22,* 579–584.

Klostermann, K., Kelley, M. L., Mignone, T., Pusateri, L., & Fals-Stewart, W. (2010). Partner violence and substance abuse: Treatment interventions. *Aggression and Violent Behavior, 15,* 162–166.

Kohl, P., Barth, R., Hazen, A., & Landsverk, J. (2005). Child welfare as a gateway to domestic violence services. *Children & Youth Services Review, 27,* 1203–1221.

Kohl, P., Edleson, J., English, D., & Barth, R. (2005). Domestic violence and pathways into child welfare services: Findings from the National Survey of Child and Adolescent Well-Being. *Children & Youth Services Review, 27,* 1167–1182.

Kohl, P., & Macy, R. (2008). Profiles of victimized women among the child welfare population: Implications for targeted child welfare policy and practices. *Journal of Family Violence, 23,* 57–68.

Krause, E. D., Kaltman, S., Goodman, L., & Dutton, M. A. (2008). Avoidant coping and PTSD symptoms related to domestic violence exposure: A longitudinal study. *Journal of Traumatic Stress, 21,* 83–90.

KwonHsieh, N., Herzig, K., Gansky, S. A., Danley, D., & Gerbert, B. (2006). Changing dentists' knowledge, attitudes, and behavior regarding domestic violence through an interactive multimedia tutorial. *Journal of the American Dental Association, 137,* 596–603.

Lapierre, S. (2008). Mothering in the context of domestic violence: The pervasiveness of a deficit model of mothering. *Child & Family Social Work, 13,* 454–463.

Lee, H. Y., Ju, E., & Lightfoot, E. (2010). The role of substance use by both perpetrators and victims in intimate partner violence outcomes. *Journal of Social Work Practice in the Addictions, 10,* 3–24.

Lichtenstein, B. (2006). Domestic violence in barriers to health care for HIV-positive women. *AIDS Patient Care & STDs, 20,* 122–132.

Lieberman, A. (2007). Ghosts and angels: Intergenerational patterns in the transmission and treatment of the traumatic sequelae of domestic violence. *Infant Mental Health Journal, 28,* 422–439.

Little, L., & Kaufman Kantor, G. (2002). Using ecological theory to understand intimate partner violence and child maltreatment. *Journal of Community Health Nursing, 19,* 133–145.

Magen, R., Conroy, K., & Del Tufo, A. (2000). Domestic violence in child welfare preventive services: Results from an intake screening questionnaire. *Children & Youth Services Review, 22,* 251–274.

Mandel, D. (2010). Child welfare and domestic violence: Tackling the themes and thorny questions that stand in the way of collaboration and improvement of child welfare practice. *Violence Against Women, 16,* 530–536.

Max, W., Rice, D. P., Finkelstein, E., Bardwell, R., & Leadbetter, S. (2004). The economic toll of intimate partner violence against women in the United States. *Violence and Victims, 19,* 259–272.

Mitchell Fuentes, C. (2008). Pathways from interpersonal violence to sexually transmitted infections: A mixed-method study of diverse women. *Journal of Women's Health, 17,* 1591–1603.

Moles, K. (2008). Bridging the divide between child welfare and domestic violence services: Deconstructing the change process. *Children & Youth Services Review, 30,* 674–688.

Mourad, M., Levendosky, A., Bogat, G., & Eye, A. (2008). Family psychopathology and perceived stress of both domestic violence and negative life events as predictors of women's mental health symptoms. *Journal of Family Violence, 23,* 661–670.

National Network to End Domestic Violence. (2009). *Domestic violence counts 2008: A 24-hour census of domestic violence shelters and services.* Washington, DC: Author.

Nelms, A. P., Gutmann, M. E., Solomon, E. A., Dewald, J. P., & Campbell, P. R. (2008). What victims of domestic violence need from the dental profession. *Journal of Dental Hygiene, 82,* 60–60.

Oliver, W., & Hairston, C. F. (2008). Intimate partner violence during the transition from prison to the community: Perspectives of incarcerated

African American men. *Journal of Aggression, Maltreatment & Trauma, 16,* 258–276.

Parker, B., McFarlane, J., & Soeken, K. (1994). Abuse during pregnancy: Effects on maternal complications and birth weight in adult and teenage women. *Obstetrics & Gynecology, 84,* 323–328.

Pinkham, S., & Malinowska-Sempruch, K. (2008). Women, harm reduction and HIV. *Reproductive Health Matters, 16,* 168–181.

Poole, N., Greaves, L., Jategaonkar, N., McCullough, L., & Chabot, C. (2008). Substance use by women using domestic violence shelters. *Substance Use & Misuse, 43,* 1129–1150.

Postmus, J., & Ortega, D. (2005). Serving two masters: When domestic violence and child abuse overlap. *Families in Society, 86,* 483–490.

Pyles, L., & Lewis, J. (2007). Women of the storm. *Affilia: Journal of Women and Social Work, 22,* 385–389.

Reese, D. (2004). Risk of domestic violence after natural disaster: Teaching research and statistics through the use of a participatory action research model. *Journal of Teaching in Social Work, 24,* 79–94.

Rivett, M., & Kelly, S. (2006). "From awareness to practice": Children, domestic violence and child welfare. *Child Abuse Review, 15,* 224–242.

Rountree, M. A., Pomeroy, E. C., & Marsiglia, F. F. (2008). Domestic violence shelters as prevention agents for HIV/AIDS? *Health & Social Work, 33,* 221–228.

Saunders, D. G., & Anderson, D. (2000). Evaluation of a domestic violence training for child protection workers and supervisors: Initial results. *Children & Youth Services Review, 22,* 373–395.

Sharps, P., Campbell, J., Campbell, D., Gary, F., & Webster, D. (2003). Risky mix: Drinking, drug use, and homicide. *NIJ Journal, 250,* 8–13.

Shlonsky, A., & Friend, C. (2007). Double jeopardy: Risk assessment in the context of child maltreatment and domestic violence. *Brief Treatment and Crisis Intervention, 7,* 253–274.

Smith, E., & Farole, D. (2009). *Profile of intimate partner violence cases in large urban counties* (NCJ 228193). Washington, DC: Bureau of Justice Statistics.

Tanskanen, A., Hintikka, J., Honkalampi, K., Haatainen, K., Koivumaa-Honkanen, H., & Viinamaki, H. (2004). Impact of multiple traumatic experiences on the persistence of depressive symptoms—A population based study. *Nordic Journal of Psychiatry, 58,* 459–464.

Teitelman, A. M., Ratcliffe, S. J., Morales-Aleman, M. M., & Sullivan, C. M. (2008). Sexual relationship power, intimate partner violence, and condom use among minority urban girls. *Journal of Interpersonal Violence, 23,* 1694–1712.

Thomas, M., & Bennett, L. (2009). The co-occurrence of substance abuse and domestic violence: A comparison of dual-problem men in substance abuse treatment and in a court-ordered batterer program. *Journal of Social Work Practice in the Addictions, 9,* 299–317.

Thurston, W., Tutty, L., Eisener, A., Lalonde, L., Belenky, C., & Osborne, B. (2009). Implementation of universal screening for domestic violence in an urgent care community health center. *Health Promotion Practice, 10,* 517–526.

Valera, E., & Berenbaum, H. (2003). Brain injury in battered women. *Journal of Consulting and Clinical Psychology, 71,* 797–804.

Visher, C., Kachnowski, V., LaVigne, N., & Travis, J. (2004). *Baltimore prisoners' experiences returning home.* Washington, DC: Urban Institute.

Visher, C., LaVigne, N., & Travis, J. (2004). *Returning home: Understanding the challenges of prisoner reentry.* Washington, DC: Urban Institute.

Warshaw, C., & Barnes, H. (2003). *Domestic violence, mental health, and trauma: Research highlights.* Chicago: Domestic Violence and Mental Health Policy Initiative.

Whitfield, C. L., Anda, R. F., Dube, S. R., & Felittle, V. J. (2003). Violent childhood experiences and the risk of intimate partner violence in adults: Assessment in a large health maintenance organization. *Journal of Interpersonal Violence, 18,* 166–185.

Williams, K., & Grant, S. (2006). Empirically examining the risk of intimate partner violence: The revised Domestic Violence Screening Instrument (DVSI–R). *Public Health Reports, 121,* 400–408.

Williams, O., Griffin, L., Davis, Y., & Bennett, L. (2006). Domestic violence, substance abuse, and child welfare: A need for collaborative, culturally competent service delivery. In R. Fong, R. McRoy, & C. Ortiz Hendricks (Eds.), *Intersecting child welfare, substance use, and family violence: Culturally competent approaches* (pp. 52–80). Alexandria, VA: Council on Social Work Education.

Wingood, G., & DiClemente, R. (1997). The effects of an abusive primary partner on the condom use and sexual negotiation practices of African American women. *American Journal of Public Health, 87,* 1016–1018.

Witte, S. S., El-Bassel, N., Gilbert, L., Wu, E., & Chang, M. (2010). Lack of awareness of partner STD risk among heterosexual couples. *Perspectives on Sexual and Reproductive Health, 42,* 49–55.

Wraith, R. (1997). Women in disaster management: Where are they? *Australian Journal of Emergency Management, 17,* 111–122.

Wyatt, G. E., Axelrod, J., Chin, D., Vargas Carmona, J., & Burns Loeb, T. (2000). Examining patterns of vulnerability to domestic violence among African American women. *Violence Against Women, 6,* 495–515.

Young, A. T., Washington, K. S., Jerman, J., & Tak, H. (2007). The Exchange Coalition—Identifying and addressing structural factors affecting HIV prevention in African American women on a national basis. *Women & Health, 46,* 131–144.

Select Resources

- *American Congress of Obstetricians and Gynecologists:* http://www.acog. org/departments/dept_notice.cfm?recno=17&bulletin=585

- *Center for a Healthy Maryland:* http://www.healthymaryland.org/domestic-violence.php

- *Child Welfare Information Gateway, U.S. Department of Health and Human Services:* http://www.childwelfare.gov/pubs/factsheets/domesticvio-lence.cfm

- *Domestic Violence and Mental Health Policy Initiative:* http://www.dvmhpi. org/CurrentProjects.htm

- *Family Violence Prevention Fund: Health Care:* http://endabuse.org/ section/programs/health_care

- *The Green Book:* http://www.thegreenbook.info/documents/Building Caps.pdf

- *Medline Plus, National Institutes of Health:* http://www.nlm.nih.gov/ medlineplus/domesticviolence.html

- *National Institute of Corrections:* http://nicic.gov/Library/022030
- *National Institute of Justice:* http://www.ojp.usdoj.gov/nij/topics/crime/child-abuse/cooccurrence.htm
- *National Center for Children in Poverty:* http://nccp.org/publications/pub_546.html
- *National Center for Trauma-Informed Care:* http://www.samhsa.gov/nctic/
- *National Center on Domestic Violence, Trauma and Mental Health:* http://www.nationalcenterdvtraumamh.org/home.php
- *National Resource Center for Permanency and Family Connections:* http://www.hunter.cuny.edu/socwork/nrcfcpp/info_services/domestic-violence-and-child-welfare.html
- *National Women's Health Information Center, U.S. Department of Health and Human Services:* http://www.womenshealth.gov/violence/
- *New York State Department of Health:* http://www.health.state.ny.us/nysdoh/rfa/hiv/guide.htm
- *Urban Institute:* http://www.urban.org/publications/406798.html
- *The Well Project:* http://www.thewellproject.org/en_US/Womens_Center/Domestic_Violence_and_HIV.jsp

Six

Just for My Girls: Intimate Partner Violence among Girls and Young Women

In this chapter, I examine issues that girls and young women face as they relate to intimate partner violence, and I identify different methods and tools needed to assess violence within this population. The consequences of domestic violence for this group are also discussed. In the Reflecting Pool, you will have an opportunity to examine your perceptions of violence in this demographic and how they affect your ability to support young girls and women. I conclude with resources that relate to teenage dating violence and campus dating violence.

Teenage Dating Violence

Teen dating violence is defined as "controlling, abusive, and aggressive behavior in a romantic relationship. It occurs in both heterosexual and homosexual relationships and can include verbal, emotional, physical, or sexual abuse or a combination of all of the above" (Dating Violence

Resource Center, 2010, ¶ 1). Dating violence is a significant problem (Hickman, Jaycox, & Aranoff, 2004). According to a Bureau of Justice Statistics report on violence against women, women and girls between the ages of 16 and 24 are at the greatest risk for experiencing intimate partner violence, rape, and sexual assault (National Center for Injury Prevention and Control, 2003; Rand, 2008; Rennison & Welchans, 2000; Tjaden & Thoennes, 2000). In fact, young women in this age group are three times more likely to experience dating violence compared with the national average. One out of every 10 high school students, male and female, have reported some form of physical abuse by an intimate partner (Grunbaum et al., 2004). Overall, 10 percent to 25 percent of high school students experience some form of dating violence (Cornelius & Resseguie, 2007). One in three teenage girls experience physical, verbal, or emotional abuse in their relationships (Davis, 2008). One in five high school girls have reported being abused by their boyfriend and between 50 percent and 80 percent of them have a friend or know someone who has experienced dating violence (O'Keefe & Trester, 1998). Nearly one in three teenage girls in ninth through 12th grade who are sexually active have reported being physically or sexually assaulted by a dating partner (Silverman, Raj, & Clements, 2004). The average age at the first abusive incident is 15, and half of the perpetrators are younger than 18. In 10 percent of cases in which a girl between the ages of 12 and 15 is murdered and in nearly 25 percent of cases in which a girl between the ages of 16 and 19 is murdered, the partner is the perpetrator. Approximately one in five tweens—young people between the ages of 11 and 14—report that they have friends in violent relationships (Liz Claiborne, 2005). Teenage dating violence is not necessarily visible in the same ways as in adult relationships. The role of technology is far more pronounced in this population. One in four teenagers experience verbal and emotional abuse through electronic means, such as cell phones and texting (National Campaign to Prevent Teen and Unplanned Pregnancy & CosmoGirl, 2008). In fact, cyberstalking has been found to occur via e-mail (83 percent) and instant messaging (35 percent). Facebook has been used as a tool to control and embarrass or shame the person via online threats, verbal abuse, use of pictures and videos, and monitoring. Continuously e-mailing or texting someone and using both as a tool to monitor or control the person is also an example of teenage dating violence. The role of technology is critical because it is something that requires monitoring and that young people need to become more aware of as a sign of dating violence.

The nature of violence escalates much faster in this population than in the adult population. Ten percent of teenagers who experience dating violence, both male and female, have been physically hurt by a partner (Eaton et al., 2008). Teenagers who have witnessed violence in the home are 50 percent more likely to experience abuse than those who have not (Wekerle et al., 2009). Both boys and girls can be victims and perpetrators of teenage dating violence. Although girls are more likely than boys to be victims of dating violence, the ways in which they experience abuse are different. For example, girls are much more likely than boys to use verbal abuse, threaten to hurt themselves, and use physical forms of abuse such as pinching, slapping, kicking, or scratching. Girls are also more likely to have an unwanted pregnancy, sexually transmitted infection, or abortion as a result of domestic violence (Deckerman & Silverman, 2005; Silverman, Raj, Mucci, & Hathaway, 2001). Boys, however, are more likely to use more severe forms of physical abuse in addition to more severe psychological abuse. A major challenge with this population is that most teenagers who experience abuse do not tell anyone. Only about 33 percent of teenagers who experience abuse share what they are experiencing with someone, and they mostly talk to friends, not mental health professionals, teachers, or police. Most parents do not talk with their children about dating violence, and many do not acknowledge or understand its prevalence in teenage life. Teenage dating violence is not just a serious problem on a short-term basis; it can also have long-term consequences (Foshee et al., 1996; Silverman et al., 2001; Smith, White, & Holland, 2003).

Patterns of abuse that start early in the life of young people often continue and become more severe as they move into adulthood. Girls who experience teenage dating violence are at a higher risk of poor academic performance, substance abuse, eating disorders, risky sexual behavior, unintended pregnancy, sexually transmitted infections, abortion, HIV, and suicide (Black & Breiding, 2008). Thus, prevention and intervention in this population is critical. The impacts of teenage dating violence are also disturbing. Teenage dating violence often increases the risk of sexual assault, sexual activity, pregnancy, sexually transmitted infections, and HIV infection, especially for female victims (Banyard & Cross, 2008; Silverman et al., 2001).

Parents are often unaware of these issues (Noonan & Charles, 2009). The reality is that many young people are involved in intimate relationships, and these relationships are occurring at younger ages than most parents realize or choose to acknowledge. Nearly three-quarters of seventh-, eighth-, and ninth-grade students report having a relationship with an intimate partner. Some parents do not take these relationships seriously, which poses an increased risk for the young person. Adults may view teenagers as having a crush or being in a phase not worthy of significant time, monitoring, and intervention, and this decision fosters relationships that are poorly monitored, insufficiently regulated, and minimally supervised.

Another unique factor related to teenage dating violence is the school environment (Mayes, 2008). Many school districts do not have policies or protocols on dating violence to protect victims experiencing abuse and address perpetrators of abuse who are still in the school and may even be in the same classroom as the victim. School districts may not have trained personnel who understand the dynamics of dating violence. Schools may not be aware of the resources in the community and may thus not be able to refer students for services. Methods of investigating acts of abuse, procedures for how to address the violence, and understanding the dynamics of abuse are all areas warranting consideration. The young person could be in a classroom with the perpetrator, who could be monitoring or controlling the person. The perpetrator could also use friends to access the survivor. It is highly possible that a young person could be experiencing abuse and teachers could be unaware of it. This situation makes it much more challenging for the young person to reach out for support, particularly if the school is not aware of or does not know how to address dating violence. If the parent has no knowledge of the relationship, the teenager may discourage adults from informing the parent about what is happening. The problem may be further compounded if the young person is in a same-sex relationship because he or she may not want to reveal his or her sexual orientation to the parent or others. Another consideration is that the parent may be unaware that the teenager is sexually active, and the teenager may not want that information to be revealed. Therefore, the nature of confidentiality becomes that much more complex with this population. Finding ways to address this issue and creating a space in which young people feel that they have someone to turn to are vitally important.

Another critical issue related to teenage dating violence is acknowledging youth culture. Because of the Internet and social media, the images that teenagers and young people are exposed to are very different from those to which other generations were exposed at the same age (Manganello et al., 2010). At times, young people are exposed to things that they may not be able to understand or contextualize. They are often exposed to music and video images that make being abusive toward and not caring about women look cool. I think that this exposure so much earlier in young people's developmental process is something that needs to be better understood not as a cause of violence but in terms of its impact on development and decision making. Teenagers' access to technology, ability to navigate the Internet, and limited supervision on these outlets often far exceed their developmental stage and can place them at risk. Understanding how to better address teenage dating violence is critical in terms of both how one relates to young people and how policies, procedures, and laws that support survivors and hold and help perpetrators of abuse are developed.

All 50 states and the District of Columbia have laws against dating violence. Educational and public systems need to be more aware of these laws and how to use them. This issue does not end in middle school or high school; it continues when young people reach their campus communities.

A Word about Culture and Teenage Dating Violence

The prevalence of intimate partner violence in the African American community has been found to be 35 percent higher than among white women and 22 percent higher than among women of other races (Tjaden & Thoennes, 2000). This trend can also be found among teenagers experiencing dating violence. African American girls in grades 9 through 12 have been found to experience physical violence in their relationship more often than girls of other races, sometimes two times more often (Davis, 2008). Almost 14 percent of African American youths report being physically assaulted by their dating partner, compared with 7 percent of white youths. The National Center for Injury Prevention and Control (2005) found that African American female youths experience teenage dating violence at a rate of 12 percent, which is the highest rate for teenage populations. Between the ages of 15 and 19, 151 African American girls per 1,000 become pregnant, compared with 132 pregnancies per 1,000 for Latina girls and 56.9 per 1,000 for white girls. The documented association between pregnancy and teenage dating violence warrants greater scrutiny of these numbers. Mexican American adolescents have experienced acculturative stress linked to their experiences with teenage dating violence (Hokoda, Galvan, Malcarne, Castaneda, & Ulloa, 2007). Teenagers of color are also more likely to use informal support networks as opposed to formal provider systems (O'Campo, Shelley, & Jaycox, 2007). An exploratory study on teenage dating violence among seventh-grade African American youths found that many of the youths reported the same perceptions of dating violence as seen in the adult literature, particularly the focus on the need to maintain privacy between couples and to not get into anyone else's business (Weisz & Black, 2008). Thus, the role of culture in teenage dating violence needs further exploration and discussion to develop better responses and systems for this population.

Characteristics to Look for in a Perpetrator of Teenage Dating Violence

- poor social skills
- poor conflict management skills
- lack of temper control
- witnessing violence at home
- gang affiliation
- engaging in criminal activity
- poor academic performance, poor attendance, or truancy
- substance use

- witnessing violence at the community level
- rigid gender role perceptions

(Foshee & Matthew, 2007; Foshee et al., 2008; Smith et al., 2003)

Campus Dating Violence

Campus dating violence affects young people across the nation regardless of the type of institution. The prevalence of campus dating violence is staggering. Nearly three-quarters of teenage and college-age women who are sexually assaulted are assaulted during their tenure in college (Fisher, Cullen, & Turner, 2000). Twenty percent to 30 percent of college students experience some form of dating violence while in college (Cornelius & Resseguie, 2007). More than 10 percent of college women experience stalking, and of those almost half are stalked by people with whom they have an intimate relationship. Most survivors report the abuse to friends and then to criminal justice professionals. Women who are raped or sexually assaulted by their intimate partner are also less likely to report the abuse than women who are raped or sexually assaulted by an unknown perpetrator.

Many parents feel a sense of relief and accomplishment when their child goes to college, because they have reached a milestone in their parental journey. It is important that parents continue to be engaged in the life of their college-age child. Being on their own, perceived as an adult, and in a relationship increases young people's vulnerability. They may not be able to get home and may feel disconnected and distant from the environment they view as secure. As young people transition into adulthood, the dynamics of the college campus are also important. Young people can be very vulnerable during this time. For most, this time is the first that they have been on their own, and the last thing they want to do is go back to a parent and say that they need help. Young people may also have limited resources or at least the perception that their resources are limited. They are developing new relationships with professors, staff, and administrators and, at the same time, with their peers. They are adjusting to their new independence and developing a better understanding of what it means to be an adult. Although there is supervision, not every moment is regulated, which can create isolation, regretful behavior, and fear of sharing what is happening with parents. The student could also be afraid of being told to come home or hearing the disappointment in the parent's or community's voice.

In addition, many universities do not have policies and procedures in place to address campus dating violence. Often, campus education efforts and relevant judicial procedures to address dating violence are limited. Survivors could very well be in class with the perpetrator. They can suffer academically because they are not going to class out of fear of seeing the perpetrator or because they are frightened by the perpetrator's presence. The judicial process may not incorporate dating violence prevention in the student code of conduct or identify investigation strategies or consequences of abuse. The victim may not report the violence. Campus police and others may not be trained in how to address dating violence. In some cases, the perpetrator could be court involved in the local jurisdiction for dating violence or criminal activities, but the college may not be aware of these court cases. The survivor could be reaching out for support services, but the college is unaware of what is happening, the perpetrator's behavior, and the risk for lethal violence and serious injury. This population also has to deal with the confidentiality issue. Having access to a perpetrator's records or revealing violence experienced by the survivor, sharing records, and reporting information to college officials are all challenges to college administrators. In addition to policies and procedures, trained personnel capable of dealing with these issues in terms of university counseling services, campus police, and judicial affairs are needed. It is important that campus officials and police understand the dynamics of dating violence so that they are able to best support victims, hold perpetrators accountable while getting help for them, and prevent dating violence through campuswide public education campaigns conducted in collaboration with student groups.

Breaking the Cycle

To break the cycle of abuse, practitioners must work with families and communities to prevent and end the violence. Practitioners can share five critical messages with their respective communities.

1. Start sending the message against dating violence and promoting healthy relationships early.

2. Open up dialogue about these kinds of sensitive issues.

3. Help the young person develop a broad support system.

4. Hold the school or university accountable for policies and procedures regarding this issue.

5. Challenge the images young people are exposed to that say that violence is normal or acceptable in a relationship.

Breaking the cycle of abuse for young people has to begin earlier. People have to begin to talk about healthy relationships at a much earlier age and not assume that every parent is having that discussion with a child. Professionals can develop developmentally appropriate tools, messages, and interventions that speak to what a healthy relationship looks like at each developmental stage. Schools can be particularly important partners in this effort by having healthy relationship education modules taught in a developmentally appropriate way in key areas of the curriculum. Indicators of abuse and risks associated with dating violence can be identified in an age-appropriate way to improve awareness of dating violence.

Parents must be more honest about the nature of the relationships that young people are entering into at younger and younger ages. It is important that parents acknowledge that many young people are in fact being exposed to more complex and more deeply involved relationships at younger ages. Practitioners also have to take these relationships seriously. This acknowledgment does not mean validating serious relationships for youths; however, adults can no longer relegate the relationship to a crush, a phase, or something the child will grow out of with time. Parents have to monitor and regulate their children's relationships and be involved in what is happening in their children's lives, recognizing that they are much more likely to first go to their peers when faced with these challenges.

Opportunities must be created for a child to develop a relationship with a trusted adult who is available to talk with that child. Sometimes a parent can be that person; at other times, the person may be another trusted adult. Parents need to think creatively about this option. They can help a child to develop healthy relationships with people in their family or trusted family friends so that the child has a pool of adults to turn to with these types of needs and questions. The parent navigates or creates some of these natural supports and resources so that the child has someone to turn to outside of peers who may be going through the same kinds of issues. Providing information to children at different points in the developmental trajectory and exposing the children to this information so they can see what dating violence looks like is important. Parents should talk to children not just about what they are experiencing, but also about what their friends are experiencing. It could be a teachable moment. It could also be an opportunity to help save the life of another child. Parents must open the dialogue with their children about this issue and, if they are uncomfortable or do not feel they have the answers, make sure that they connect their children with people in both their natural environment and formal provider networks who can supply them with the answers and the resources they need. Young people should be asked to identify their trusted adults. They should know to whom they can turn and to whom they can go for unconditional support. Parents should also explain that what appears to be judgment may actually be the person showing that he or she cares and is concerned but not placing value on what is happening. Young people must feel that an adult is invested in them, cares about them, values them, and respects them. They also need models of healthy relationships to emulate within their families and committees. Young people must be reminded that change comes from within and that no one can change another person. They must be armed with a sense of goals and purpose so that they can begin to understand the negative impact violence can have on their dreams and ambitions.

Parents can also be better engaged in their children's education on this issue during academic hours and in after-school programs. Parents should ask how dating violence is identified and addressed at their child's academic institution. They should inquire as to protocols and accountable people, in addition to examining the student code of conduct regarding these issues. Parents can play a really important and active role in this process, but other adults can be a part of the process too. Faith-based groups, civic organizations, grassroots organizations, fraternities, sororities, and individuals can also be engaged to promote dating violence prevention education and promote healthy relationship education throughout the developmental trajectory.

They can also create positive countermessages within the community that promote healthy relationships.

Young people must be helped to understand the messages in music and on-screen images so that they can make sense out of what they are being exposed to. Fully censoring these images is increasingly challenging. Therefore, parents must be more aware of what their children are listening to and watching (including video games). Parents must be willing to challenge and be challenged regarding the messages provided in the music and by performers, actors, and other celebrities who provide negative examples. One very public example of this issue was the domestic violence revealed in the relationship of two musicians. Young people, before hearing the story, were quick to support the perpetrator and blame the survivor for the violence, despite the very visible and debilitating signs of physical abuse. Although this situation was awful, it also provided a teachable moment for parents to advance the conversation about dating violence. Subsequent music left young people even more conflicted, trying to understand whether women do want to be abused. At times, adults can be dismissive of these questions and concerns; instead, they need to talk with young people about these issues and help them to better understand what is happening and why it may be occurring.

Reflecting Pool

In this chapter, I discussed the complexity of teenage dating violence and campus dating violence. Both require increased focus and attention by family and friends, practitioners, and school and university systems. I would like you to consider your perceptions of teenage and campus dating violence and how they affect your ability to work with this population.

My Reflection

I can remember one of the first times I was confronted with an issue of teenage dating violence. The young woman was 16 years old and in a relationship with a 17-year-old. Her mother did not know that she was sexually active in the relationship and did not approve of the boy, but the girl continued to see him anyway. As time passed, the boy became more controlling—telling her where to go and what to do. She was afraid to tell her mother about the relationship. When her boyfriend became physically abusive, she continued to be silent. She did not tell her friends what she was experiencing because she was embarrassed and confused. She shared that she had fought back and so did not see the abuse as domestic violence, but she knew she was unhappy in the relationship and afraid of what could happen next. Months went by, and she told her boyfriend's mother about the abuse. Her boyfriend's mother shared that she was experiencing abuse at the hands of his father but that, in time, the girl would get used to it and it would not be a big deal. What was challenging for me was that throughout the entire ordeal, none of her friends or family knew about the violence and the one adult she told reinforced and validated it. I realized then that greater education and awareness was needed, as well as more voices to guide and support young people if they were confronted with this issue.

Your Reflection

- What are your thoughts about teenage dating violence and campus dating violence?

- How can young people be encouraged to report and receive support if confronted with abuse?

- What is your comfort level with talking with young people about this issue and using the technology to support them?

- What can adults do to better educate and support young people on this issue?

- What is your value base in terms of when you believe a young person should be allowed into a relationship or have a sexual relationship, and how does that affect your working with the young person?

Notes:

_____

_____

_____

_____
_____
_____
_____
_____
_____
_____
_____
_____
_____

References

Banyard, V. L., & Cross, C. (2008). Consequences of teen dating violence: Understanding intervening variables in ecological context. *Violence Against Women, 14,* 998–1013.

Black, M. C., & Breiding, M. J. (2008). Adverse health conditions and health risk behaviors associated with intimate partner violence. *Morbidity and Mortality Weekly Report, 57,* 113–117.

Cornelius, T. L., & Resseguie, N. (2007). Primary and secondary prevention programs for dating violence: A review of the literature. *Aggression and Violent Behavior, 12,* 364–375.

Dating Violence Resource Center. (2010). *Teen dating violence* [Fact sheet]. Retrieved from http://www.ncvc.org/dvrc

Davis, A. (2008). Interpersonal and physical dating violence among teens. *The National Council on Crime and Delinquency Focus.* Retrieved from www.nccd-crc.org/nccd/pubs/2008_focus_teen_dating_violence.pdf

Decker, M., Silverman, J., & Raj, A. (2005). Dating violence and sexually transmitted disease/HIV testing and diagnosis among adolescent females. *Pediatrics, 116,* 272–276.

Eaton, D. K., Kann, L., Kinchen, S., Shanklin, S., Ross, J., Hawkins, J., et al. (2008). Youth risk behavioral surveillance—United States, 2007. *Morbidity and Mortality Weekly Report, 57,* 1–131.

Fisher, B., Cullen, F., & Turner, M. (2000). *The sexual victimization of college women* (NCJ 182369). Washington, DC: Bureau of Justice Statistics.

Foshee, V. A., Karriker-Jaffe, K. J., Reyes, H., Ennett, S., Suchindran, C., Bauman, K., & Benefield, T. (2008). What accounts for demographic differences in trajectories of adolescent dating violence? An examination of intrapersonal and contextual mediators. *Journal of Adolescent Health, 42,* 596–604.

Foshee, V. A., Linder, G. F., Bauman, K. E., Langwick, S. A., Arriaga, X. B., Heath, J. L., et al. (1996). The Safe Dates Project: Theoretical basis, evaluation design, and selected baseline findings. *American Journal of Preventive Medicine, 12,* 39–47.

Foshee, V. A., & Matthew, R. (2007). Adolescent dating violence perpetration: A review of findings, methodological limitations, and suggestions for future research. In D. J. Flannery, A. T. Vazjoni, & I. D. Waldman (Eds.), *The Cambridge handbook of violent behavior and aggression* (pp. 431–449). New York: Cambridge University Press.

Grunbaum, J., Kann, L., Kinchen, S., Ross, J., Hawkins, J., Lowry, R., et al. (2004). Youth risk behavior surveillance—United States, 2003. *Morbidity and Mortality Weekly Report, 53,* 1–96.

Hickman, L., Jaycox, L., & Aranoff, J. (2004). Domestic violence among adolescents: Prevalence, gender distribution and prevention program effectiveness. *Trauma, Violence & Abuse, 5,* 123–142.

Hokoda, A., Galvan, D., Malcarne, V., Castaneda, D., & Ulloa, E. (2007). An exploratory study examining teen dating violence, acculturation, and acculturative stress in Mexican-American adolescents. *Journal of Aggression, Maltreatment & Trauma, 14,* 33–49.

Liz Claiborne, Inc. (2005). *Omnibuzz topline findings: Teen relationship abuse research, teenage research unlimited.* Retrieved from http://www.loveisnotabuse.com/surveyresults.htm

Manganello, J., Henderson, V., Jordan, A., Trentacoste, N., Martin, S., Hennessy, M., & Fishbein, M. (2010). Adolescent judgement of sexual content on television: Implications for future content analysis research. *Journal of Sex Research, 47,* 364–373.

Mayes, T. (2008). Students with no-contact orders against abusive classmates: Recommendations for educators. *Preventing School Failure, 52,* 37–44.

National Campaign to Prevent Teen and Unplanned Pregnancy and Cosmo-Girl.com. (2008). *Sex and tech: Results from a survey of teens and young adults.* Retrieved from http://www.thenationalcampaign.org/sextech/PDF/SexTech-Summary.pdf

National Center for Injury Prevention and Control. (2003). *Costs of intimate partner violence against women in the United States.* Atlanta: Author.

Noonan, R., & Charles, D. (2009). Developing teen dating violence prevention strategies. *Violence Against Women, 15,* 1087–1105.

O'Campo, B., Shelley, G., & Jaycox, L. (2007). Latino teens talk about help seeking and help giving in relation to dating violence. *Violence Against Women, 13,* 172–189.

O'Keefe, M., & Trester, L. (1998). Victims of dating violence among high school students. *Violence Against Women, 4,* 195–223.

Rand, M. (2008). *Criminal victimization, 2007* (NCJ 224390). Washington, DC: Bureau of Justice Statistics.

Rennison, C. M., & Welchans, S. (2000). *Intimate partner violence* (BJS Special Report No. NCJ 178247), Washington, DC: U.S. Department of Justice.

Silverman, J., Raj, A., & Clements, K. (2004). Dating violence and associated sexual risk and pregnancy among adolescent girls in the United States. *Pediatrics, 114,* 220–225.

Silverman, J., Raj, A., Mucci, I., & Hathaway, J. (2001). Dating violence against adolescent girls and associated substance use, unhealthy weight control, sexual risk behavior, pregnancy, and suicidality. *JAMA, 286,* 572–579.

Smith, P. H., White, J. W., & Holland, I. J. (2003). A longitudinal perspective on dating violence among adolescent and college-age women. *American Journal of Public Health, 93,* 1104–1109.

Tjaden, P., & Thoennes, N. (2000). *Extent, nature and consequences of violence against women: Findings from the National Violence Against Women Survey* (NCJ 181867). Washington, DC: Bureau of Justice Statistics.

Weisz, A., & Black, B. (2008). Peer intervention in dating violence: Beliefs of African American middle school adolescents. *Journal of Ethnic and Cultural Diversity in Social Work, 17,* 177–196.

Wekerle, C., Leung, E., Wall, A. M., MacMillan, H., Boyle, M., Trocme, N., & Waechter, R. (2009). The contribution of childhood emotional abuse to teen dating violence among child protective services-involved youth. Child Abuse & Neglect, 33, 45–58.

Select Resources

- *Advocates for Youth:* http://www.advocatesforyouth.org/index.php?option=com_content&task=view&id=417&Itemid=177

- *Aequitas: The Prosecutors' Resource on Violence Against Women:* http://www.aequitasresource.org/

- *Break the Cycle:* http://www.breakthecycle.org/

- *Centers for Disease Control and Prevention:* http://www.cdc.gov/violenceprevention/intimatepartnerviolence/teen_dating_violence.html

- *Dating Violence Resource Center:* http://www.ncvc.org/ncvc/main.aspx?dbID=DB_DatingViolenceResourceCenter101

- *Family Violence Prevention Fund:* http://www.thatsnotcool.com/

- *National Teen Dating Abuse Helpline:* http://www.loveisrespect.org/

- *Red Flag Campaign:* http://www.theredflagcampaign.org/

- *Runaway and Homeless Youth and Relationship Violence Toolkit:* http://www.nrcdv.org/rhydvtoolkit/

- *The Safe Space.org:* http://www.thesafespace.org/the-basics/in-your-community/domestic-and-dating-violence-on-campus/

- *Teen Dating Violence Prevention Project:* http://www.teendvmonth.org/

- *U.S. Department of Education, Higher Education Center:* http://www.higheredcenter.org/resources/campus-dating-violence-fact-sheet

- *You Love Me You, Love Me Not:* http://www.youlovemeyoulovemenot.org/

Seven

The Perpetrator of Abuse: The Not-So-Obvious Guy Next Door

In this chapter, I focus on better understanding perpetrators of abuse and identify characteristics and typologies of perpetrators of intimate partner violence. Emerging issues related to perpetration of abuse are discussed. The Reflecting Pool will challenge you to think about and understand your perception of perpetrators of abuse and how it affects how you work with perpetrators and survivors of abuse. At the end of the chapter, resources are identified in relation to services for perpetrators of abuse.

Typologies and Characteristics of Perpetrators

You cannot identify a perpetrator by looking at him or her. Even as I identify typologies of battering, it is important to understand that an individual may be a perpetrator but still not fit a typology. A big misconception is that a person can look at someone and know that he or she is a perpetrator of abuse. At times, the red flags will be evident and will clearly indicate that the person is a perpetrator of abuse. At other times, the perpetrator will be the not-so-obvious "guy next door."

It is important again to emphasize that people cannot look at someone and know that the person is or is not a perpetrator of abuse. When looking at and considering the characteristics or typologies of perpetrators, put them in context. A critical point to remember is that practitioners have seen enough perpetrators of abuse to understand that they have certain characteristics, which are categorized into typologies (Bender & Roberts, 2007; Chifriller & Hennessy, 2006; Lohr, Bonge, Witte, Hamberger, & Langhinrichsen-Rohling, 2005). Although practitioners have an understanding of where a person fits within a typology, it does not mean that they understand the type of intervention that will best serve the person (Chiffriller & Hennessy, 2006). Increasing attention is being paid to better understanding the typologies and how they connect with interventions.

Before I discuss the typologies, it is most important to remember that perpetrating domestic violence is a choice, no matter the person's profile. Although professionals examine these characteristics, they should be sure to remember that no matter what the person's characteristics are, he or she has still made the choice to use abusive behaviors to control and use power over another person to achieve a desired outcome. The other issue to consider is the idea of change. Although the perpetrator makes the choice to abuse, he also has the capacity to change if he chooses to do so. However, at no time does the survivor have the responsibility or the power to change the perpetrator's behavior. The perpetrator is responsible for making a change in his behavior that will determine his success and ability to benefit from services received. The idea that a perpetrator of abuse cannot change should not be the guiding philosophy (Aymer, 2008; Bennett & Williams, 2001; Bent-Goodley, 2005). That said, although I believe in the idea of hope and the possibility that someone can make different choices and decisions, that does not mean I do not hold the person accountable for the behavior. Social workers have to believe in the possibility of change while being realistic and holding the person accountable.

Typologies

Understanding the typologies can give you a better indication of perpetrators' potential behaviors and how to best intervene with them (Stoops, Bennett, & Vincent, 2010). Although we have not gotten to the point at which behavior can be fully predicted, the typologies provide professionals with clues as to how to conduct safety planning with survivors and how to best intervene with perpetrators. It is also important to recognize that battering is a continuum on which the level of duration and severity of violence can range from low to high (Roberts, 2007). Therefore, a person may meet the risk standards for the first typology but escalate to those for the third typology on the basis of behavior. Professionals should look for such changes during ongoing risk assessments. Perpetrators of abuse usually fall into one of three typologies. These typologies are organized around the severity and frequency of abuse, the general nature of the abuse, and the degree to which the perpetrator may have psychological or psychiatric issues.

Table 7-1: Typologies

Typology 1 (Lower Risk)	Typology 2 (Moderate Risk)	Typology 3 (High Risk)
• Violence in home only • Low frequency • Low severity • Verbally or psychologically abusive	• Passive–aggressive • Dependent • Compulsive or borderline personality disorder • Moderate level of severity of violence • Generally violent	• Violent inside or outside of the home • Antisocial personality disorder • Severe psychopathology • Emotional volatility • Severe violence • High levels of anger and jealousy • Frequent violence

Sources: Corvo (2006); Holtzworth-Munroe, Meehan, Herron, Rehman, & Stuart (2003); Holtzworth-Munroe & Stuart (1994); Stanford, Houston, & Baldridge (2008); Tilley, Rugari, & Walker (2008); White & Gondolf (2000).

Most perpetrators of abuse fall into three typologies: (1) type 1, low risk; (2) type 2, moderate risk; and (3) type 3, high risk. Perpetrators who fall into the low-risk category are men who have perpetrated violence in the family, not men engaged in violent acts and violent behavior outside of the home. Other characteristics of a low-risk typology are that the person does not have a serious mental illness, typically does not have a criminal background, and engages in what would be considered a low-level severity and a low frequency of violence. It is important to not equate lesser frequency of abuse with a lower severity level. A person who falls into this typology may be characterized by the use of verbal and emotional abuse and be someone who is not highly conflictual outside of the home and does not evidence pathological behavior.

Perpetrators who fall into the moderate risk category show passive–aggressive behaviors and are emotionally dependent on the partner. They could have a compulsive or borderline personality disorder. They evidence a moderate level of severity and a moderate frequency of violence and are not typically engaged in criminal activity or violent activity outside of the home.

Perpetrators who fall into the high-risk category generally evidence violent and antisocial behaviors. They engage in violent behavior outside of the home, likely have a criminal record, and show high levels of psychopathology. They may have borderline personality disorder, narcissistic personality disorder, or other kinds of mental illness. I want to caution you against equating mental illness with being a perpetrator of abuse. Clearly, most people who have mental illness are not abusive. A perpetrator may have a high level of mental illness, increasing the level of risk, but mental illness is not a cause of domestic violence.

Characteristics

Regardless of typology, the following are characteristics and traits to look for in perpetrators of abuse: a person who

- is controlling your behavior, actions, or choices
- lashes out with abusive language
- may seem charming around others but the total opposite when you are alone

- is close minded and does not value your opinion
- feels that his decision is final
- has very rigid gender roles
- seems unpredictable
- is jealous of your friends, family, your achievements, and others being around you
- justifies his violent and abusive behavior
- has a history of violence or abuse toward women

Batterers Intervention and Treatment

At one time, perpetrators of abuse were largely referred for services from within their communities. These men could turn to individuals, organizations, or community groups for referrals. Currently, most men receiving batterers intervention program (BIP) services are referred from the court and required to attend BIPs that often vary in focus and length. BIPs have had modest success in stemming future violence (Babcock, Green, & Robie, 2004; Gondolf, 2007). They begin with the premise that perpetration of violence is intentional and used to control the partner (Goetz, Shackelford, Romero, Kaighobadi, & Miner, 2008). Most programs are from 12 to 52 weeks long and have an educational or therapeutic focus (Gondolf, 2007; Rothman, Butchart, & Cerda, 2003). BIPs focus on challenging gender role perceptions, building nonviolent skills, addressing issues of power and control, holding the perpetrator accountable for choices and behaviors, maintaining victim safety, and providing anger management skills (Healey, Smith, & O'Sullivan, 1998). Some programs have expanded to also address the objectification and negative views of women, conflict resolution skills, social and familial factors, denial and minimization of abuse, gender role stress, and feelings of insecurity and mistrust (Catlett, Toews, & Walilko, 2010; Jakupcak, Lisak, & Roemer, 2002; Tilley & Brackley, 2005). The need to ensure that these groups cover more than patriarchy and sexism is critical. It is important that men understand how institutional sexism and patriarchy feed into sexist practices and behaviors. At the same time, BIPs must also provide educational groups to address stereotypes about women, mental health challenges, men's exposure to family and community violence, cultural and social factors affecting men, substance abuse, and negotiating daily stress, particularly gender-related stress (Aymer, 2008; Bent-Goodley, Rice, Williams, & Pope, 2011; Corvo, Dutton, & Wan-Yi, 2009; Dalton, 2009; Huss, Covell, & Langhinrichsen-Rohling, 2006; Thomas & Bennett, 2009; Whitfield, Anda, Dube, & Felitti, 2003). The dearth of services available to men, particularly primary prevention services, must also be recognized. It is critical that services be provided to men and boys on a continuum ranging from primary to tertiary prevention. Few gender-specific services are available to men to help them generate strategies to deal with overwhelming emotions, manage arguments and stress, deal with the pressures of life, and address self-doubt and low self-esteem (Fenton & Rathus, 2010). Early detection screening mechanisms are needed before the perpetration of abuse is manifested (Tilley et al., 2008). These issues do not remove accountability from the perpetrator or provide a justification for the choice the perpetrator makes to be abusive. Social workers are taught to provide services for clients where they are at. As part of providing these services, social workers can target issues to make services more efficient and effective. Ultimately, the success of these services benefits the perpetrator, the survivor, the children, the family and community, and future partners. Therefore, identifying how best to assist someone, regardless of what the person has done, benefits many people. Efforts in this area are particularly important because women often choose to stay with the partner. In that situation, it is even more important that providers develop effective strategies to hold men accountable, treat them effectively, and keep women safe.

Cultural Context of Batterers Intervention Programs

All BIPs are required to hold the perpetrator accountable. Yet, while holding men of color accountable, it is critical to understand the oppression and discrimination they experience (Bell & Mattis, 2000; Carrillo & Tello,

2008; Gondolf & Williams, 2001; Hancock & Siu, 2009; Williams & Becker, 1994). To work most effectively with this population, it is critical that the cultural context and historical and contemporary experiences with racism and discrimination be incorporated into work with the perpetrator. Men of color have suffered varying forms of discrimination and oppression not experienced by white men. These forms of oppression are real and have specific consequences for relationships among people of color (Almeida & Dolan-Delvecchio, 1999; Belknap, 2007; Bent-Goodley, Rice, Williams, & Pope, 2011; Bent-Goodley & Williams, 2008; Carrillo & Tello, 2008; Gondolf, 2007; Saez-Betacourt, Lam, & Nguyen, 2008; Smith, 2008; Williams, Oliver, & Pope, 2008). Some of the ways that cultural context affects social workers' ability to engage perpetrators of abuse follow:

- The historical context of the helping relationship is critical. Men of color do not view social service systems as being places where they can traditionally seek and obtain assistance or support. Thus, social service systems are not viewed as helpful places, but rather as places for women and children to obtain support or places where men are discounted and not viewed as important to the family system.

- Men of color often mistrust formal provider systems. Formal providers are not viewed as wanting to help men and are more associated with manipulating men and being dishonest in wanting to assist men with issues. The Tuskegee syphilis experiment is one example; a community of men was told they were being treated for syphilis when, in fact, they were not being treated but instead observed to see how syphilis would affect them. This study took place many years ago; however, it is still identified as an example of how formal systems view and treat people of color, particularly men of color.

- Understanding the lack of cultural competence in how social workers respond to domestic violence with perpetrators of abuse is also critical. A lack of cultural competence results in poor cross-cultural communication in which the use and meaning of language is not understood. Understanding people's language, how language is used, and the meaning of language is basic to helping anyone. Without this fundamental understanding, miscommunication is pronounced, and there is an inability to understand how to best and most effectively help the person. The perception of not being understood can affect how people receive services and their willingness to be engaged and invested in the program. In addition, resistance to and lack of willingness to create programming that supports men's cultural context creates a feeling that the provider does not understand their reality and, thus, cannot truly help them to overcome the use of violence. Coming to a white provider to get help with these very personal and intimate issues is also very challenging. Not understanding the difficulty of asking for assistance from someone who may be viewed as an oppressive force is a dire mistake. Just being able to overcome this issue could be a challenge for the person. In addition, not seeing providers and administrators who reflect the population is a challenge. Having more men of color in positions throughout the program structure builds a sense of being understood and comfort that perhaps the organization is identifying and adequately addressing the population's issues. Of course, just having a person of color on staff is not enough. The person of color has to be culturally competent, and the institute has to be committed to manifesting an understanding of cultural context in the organization's practices and policies.

- Not addressing the cultural context results in the perception that the services are not relevant and helpful. Perpetrators then become disconnected from the services and the service provider and doubtful of the service provider's ability to address the issues that have meaning in their lives. Providers essentially have to go beyond the idea that they are just there to address the man's perpetration of violence. They have to recognize that to challenge and change the man's choice to be abusive they have to be committed to helping the man with issues that go beyond the violence. Being able to address these issues not only helps to build trust, but also allows for greater accountability for the man's choices as the reality of his situation and experiences come to light.

- Because of historical and contemporary discrimination, men of color also require additional concrete services, such as assistance with obtaining employment, housing, job training, and economic support.

One can still hold the man accountable for his behavior while providing connections to these concrete services.

A blended perspective is needed to best serve and support the needs of men of color who have perpetrated violence. A blended perspective in batterers treatment allows the provider to address the cultural context of the perpetrator's life experiences while simultaneously holding the perpetrator accountable for his behavior and choice to use violence in the relationship (Williams, 2008; Williams et al., 2008). The blended perspective helps to increase accessibility, blend and incorporate cultural knowledge and awareness into intervention and services, and encourage greater community awareness and participation in treatment.

Emerging Issues

Issues connected with BIPs have emerged in recent years. Two particular issues receiving increased attention are (1) fatherhood and domestic violence and (2) child custody and domestic violence. I explore these two issues as they relate to the perpetration of abuse.

Fatherhood and Perpetrators of Abuse

Practitioners must understand the connection between fatherhood programs and perpetrators of abuse from three perspectives: (1) the connection between fatherhood and domestic violence movements, (2) the relationship between parents after abuse, and (3) the relationship between the father and the child after abuse.

Fatherhood and Domestic Violence Movements

The question is compelling: "To what degree should a man be involved in parenting after abuse?" In 30 percent to 60 percent of cases in which a man is abusive toward his partner, child abuse and neglect also occur (Chipungu & Bent-Goodley, 2004; Little & Kaufman Kantor, 2002). The father's presence in the child's life, although critical, warrants considerable attention when the father is also a perpetrator of abuse. It is important to distinguish between the fathers' rights movement and the fatherhood movement. The fathers' rights movement has stressed the importance of father engagement regardless of whether fathers have shown violent behavior. Fathers' rights groups are mostly concerned with fathers having access to their children, which can be detrimental to the children and the family. The fatherhood movement is primarily concerned with the development of fathers, improved fathering, and men's ability to provide support and play an integral role in their families. Fatherhood programs within the fatherhood movement can be wonderful allies in domestic violence prevention and have already begun to collaborate with domestic violence programs. Fatherhood programs can cosponsor BIPs, represent fathers' needs, assist with recruitment and retention, reinforce nonviolent and positive behaviors, and support healthy fathering and respect for women in relationships (Boggess, May, & Roulet, 2007). They can be available to support program goals and objectives outside of office hours and in communities outside of traditional program hours. Good fatherhood programs emphasize manhood development, which includes promoting nonviolent and nonabusive relationships and improved ways of building stronger families and communities. They can further the work with a wider audience and are often respected entities in their communities, which can further the reach and impact of domestic violence programs.

Relationship between Parents after Abuse

The woman may not want to maintain a relationship with the perpetrator because of her own fear and anger about the situation. Some women may be compelled to continue communicating with the perpetrator because of the children's perceived need or because of the fear of raising the children alone. This issue has been particularly relevant to women raising male children and the desire to have the father present to support boys' navigating dangerous communities and negotiate challenges specific to boys and men. This challenge is very complex because the woman, while recognizing her own safety issues, may be compelled to involve the perpetrator in the family for what she perceives as the child's best interest. If there is a risk to the child, social workers are required to act. If there is no risk to the child, they are still called to act on the basis of the profession's ethical principles. Practitioners must recognize both the formal and the informal arrangements survivors make to support their children from their perspective. Although social workers may not see the value of the perpetrator in the home because of the violence, their role is to discuss choices, explore viable options, and reinforce healthy and safe choices.

Relationship between the Father and the Child

Practitioners are faced with the question of how to help women stay safe in these situations while also ensuring the children's safety and well-being. They must also consider and value the child's perception and desire for a relationship with the father (Cater, 2007). The child may feel conflicted—wanting the relationship, not wanting the relationship, feeling angry with the father, identifying with the father, and being confused about going back and forth between these feelings. If the relationship was poor, then the child may want no relationship with the father.

The perpetrator needs to learn how to engage in healthy parenting (Featherstone & Peckover, 2007). He needs to readjust his focus to the children's needs, not his own needs and desires (Francis & Wolfe, 2008). He has to learn how to build new relationships with his children (Fleck-Henderson & Arean, 2004). He must also realize that the responsibility to develop, redevelop, or change the nature of the relationship rests with him. Practitioners must provide these men with the tools to do so while maintaining a consistent vigilance toward accountability and maintaining the safety of the mother and the child. Some men do not need to be in contact with their children if they pose a threat to the physical and mental well-being of the children. Better tools are needed to help make that determination, and if a child has expressed concern and apprehension in connection with the father, then that should be honored.

Child Custody Issues

Child custody is a major issue in cases of domestic violence. Determining the structure and nature of parenting arrangements after the identification of domestic violence is a major concern for the children, survivor, and families associated with the situation. Fathers' rights advocates and domestic violence advocates have debated the best way to determine child custody after domestic violence has been identified. Fathers' rights advocates state that fathers are often automatically denied custody and that it might still be in the child's best interest to maintain a relationship with the father despite the violence. Domestic violence advocates state that the father's violence against the mother could pose risks to both the child and the mother and that forced interaction with the father could be detrimental to the child's emotional well-being. There continues to be a desire to promote mediation and joint custody despite the identification of domestic violence (Jaffe & Crooks, 2004). The need to preserve the safety of survivors and children is central to developing more comprehensive and effective assessment tools that go beyond psychological testing and the identification of physical violence (Stark, 2009; Zorza, 2009). Without a comprehensive assessment of families' full needs, risks, and protective mechanisms, the possibility of revictimization of survivors and children will be increased (Jaffe, Crooks, & Wolfe, 2003). The need for more adequate training and resources, greater collaboration with community partners, parenting plans that optimize strengths and address weaknesses, and awareness efforts that target the identification of attitudes toward and beliefs about domestic violence has been identified as crucial (Jaffe et al., 2003; Morrill, Jianyu, Dunn, Sung, & Smith, 2005; Stahly, 2007). These issues are particularly important because fewer than one-half of state child custody laws have specific provisions in place related to domestic violence and child custody. One mechanism that has been used to respond to these issues is the use of supervised visitation centers to preserve the survivor's safety and maintain the child's relationship with the father. Supervised visitation centers provide scheduled contact and a structured environment in which to facilitate child–parent interactions, a safe exchange location for the child, and a means to allow the survivor's residence to remain unknown to the perpetrator. These centers also allow women to share potential concerns about risks for further violence and to obtain supports for the child, including parenting education (Stern & Oehme, 2007). Supervised visitation staff require training in domestic violence so that they are able to identify when children are being manipulated by the perpetrator or negatively affected by visits with the father, when false allegations are being made about parenting, when survivors are being threatened, and when stalking may be occurring (Oehme & Maxwell, 2004). Protective orders should also be identified and discussed with supervised visitation staff and in collaboration with community partners to ensure that needed supports are provided to the entire family to ensure safety and well-being. The role of culture in supervised visitation centers is also critical. Culturally based parenting practices should be acknowledged. The appearance of the center should encompass diverse populations, and ensuring that providers are trained to engage and work with people of diverse faiths is critical to the success of this model, as is enforcement of child custody arrangements while maintaining a relationship with the indigenous community.

Reflecting Pool

In this chapter, I have sought to help you better understand the characteristics of perpetrators of abuse and the services most often used to address the abuse. I have also discussed fatherhood and child custody as issues that continue to be discussed and debated in the literature and in the field as they relate to perpetrators of abuse. I have sought to challenge your ideas about what a perpetrator of abuse looks like and how the person's choice to be abusive affects the entire family unit. Now, in the Reflecting Pool, I challenge you to consider your perspectives on the perpetration of abuse and how they affect your ability to work with and engage this population.

My Reflection

As a new social worker, my first case of domestic violence initially had nothing to do with abuse. In fact, the family came to the agency for play therapy because one of their children was having outbursts in class and behaving aggressively toward the other children. I began play therapy and then began parenting education with the parents to reinforce what was being done during the play therapy session. I found in these sessions that the father did all the talking and the mother sat quietly, saying nothing. When I asked for her opinion, she would defer to her husband. One day, I asked if I could meet with them separately. The father challenged me about the need to meet separately and stated that his wife was not comfortable with the idea because she had problems expressing herself. He explained that she had developed a speech disorder after falling and hitting her head. All these were clues that domestic violence might be occurring. Not realizing this, I continued to work with the parents until one day the mother came alone. Her husband had to work and confidently decided to send her alone, thinking she would not reveal the violence she was experiencing. On that occasion, she shared with me everything that was happening. Her speech disorder was the direct result of a traumatic brain injury. She detailed incidents of being hit with an iron, beaten with cords, and repeatedly chastised in front of the children. She explained that she wanted to leave the relationship, but that her family could not understand why she would leave such a wonderful man. Her husband was the sole provider, and from their perspective, he was taking care of his family and a wife who had a special need. This man had manipulated everyone in her life, including me. He eventually went into a BIP. He accepted no responsibility for his behavior, and he blamed her for his having to assume the role of sole provider, not accepting responsibility for the fact that his behavior had caused her disability. Then he blamed his behavior on his excessive drinking. A year later, he finally stated that he abused his wife because he could. He detailed why and how he controlled her and began to accept responsibility for his behavior. I wish I could tell you how this story ended, but the family moved out of our catchment area and transferred to another program. What I can tell you is that perpetrators of abuse, regardless of co-occurring issues, are very conscious of how and why they inflict abuse on their partners. Practitioners have to be vigilant to and aware of the signs of abuse. Someone once told me that the vigilance can sometimes lead to a practitioner seeing everything as domestic violence. From my perspective, social workers constantly assess and reassess client situations. Part of that process includes being aware of potential indicators of various issues. Domestic violence is one of those issues. Perpetrators rely on practitioners' not being informed or aware of the indicators and not being vigilant in their efforts. It is critical that social workers be informed and aware of how to identify and respond to these issues.

Your Reflection

- Do you believe that perpetrators of abuse have the capacity to change?
- Have you ever defended a perpetrator?
- Do you believe that some women provoke abuse?
- How do you respond to others when they blame the victim?
- Do you believe that men who have been abusive should have no further access to their children?
- Do you believe that parents can work together to raise their children after abuse has occurred?

Notes:

_____

_____

_____

_____

_____

_____

_____

_____

_____

_____

References

Almeida, R. V., & Dolan-Delvecchio, K. (1999). Addressing Culture in Batterers Intervention: The Asian Indian community as an illustrative example. *Violence Against Women, 5,* 654–683.

Aymer, S. (2008). Beyond power and control: Clinical interventions with men engaged in partner abuse. *Clinical Social Work Journal, 36,* 323–332.

Babcock, J., Green, C., & Robie, C. (2004). Does batterers treatment work? A meta-analytic review of domestic violence treatment. *Clinical Psychology Review, 23,* 1023–1053.

Belknap, J. (2007). Culturally-focused batterer counseling [Editorial]. *Criminology & Public Policy, 6,* 337–340.

Bell, C. C., & Mattis, J. (2000). The importance of cultural competence in ministering to African American victims of domestic violence. *Violence Against Women, 6,* 515–532.

Bender, K., & Roberts, A. R. (2007). Battered women versus male batterer typologies: Same or different based on evidence-based studies? *Aggression and Violent Behavior, 12,* 519–530.

Bennett, L., & Williams, O. J. (2001). Substance abuse and men who batter: Issues in theory and practice. *Violence Against Women, 9,* 558–575.

Bent-Goodley, T. B. (2005). An African-centered approach to domestic violence. *Families in Society, 86,* 197–206.

Bent-Goodley, T. B., Rice, J., Williams, O. J., & Pope, M. (2011). Services for perpetrators of abuse: A critique and emerging directions. In M. P. Koss, J. White, & A. Kazdin (Eds.), *Violence against women and children: Consensus, critique and emerging directions* (pp. 199–214). Washington, DC: American Psychological Association.

Bent-Goodley, T. B., & Williams, O. J. (2008). *Community insights on domestic violence among African Americans: Conversations about domestic violence and other issues affecting their community, Detroit, Michigan.* St. Paul, MN: Institute on Domestic Violence in the African American Community.

Boggess, J., May, R., & Roulet, M. (2007, June). *Collaboration and partnership: Fatherhood practitioners and advocates against domestic violence working together to serve women, men and families.* Madison, WI: Center for Family Policy and Practice.

Carrillo, R., & Tello, J. (Eds.). (2008). *Family violence and men of color: Healing the wounded male spirit* (2nd ed.). New York: Springer.

Cater, A. (2007). Children's meaning-conciliation of their fathers' violence related to fathers and violence in general. *Journal of Scandinavian Studies in Criminology and Crime Prevention, 8,* 41–55.

Catlett, B. S., Toews, M. L., & Walilko, V. (2010). Men's gendered constructions of intimate partner violence as predictors of court-mandated batterer treatment drop out. *American Journal of Community Psychology, 45,* 107–123.

Chiffriller, S. H., & Hennessy, J. J. (2006). Male batterer profiles: Support for an empirically generated typology. *Journal of Offender Rehabilitation, 44,* 117–131.

Chipungu, S. S., & Bent-Goodley, T. B. (2004). Challenges of contemporary foster care: Ensuring safe, stable and supportive homes for children. *Future of Children, 14,* 75–94.

Corvo, K. (2006). Violence, separation, and loss in the families of origin of domestically violent men. *Journal of Family Violence, 21,* 117–125.

Corvo, K., Dutton, D., & Wan-Yi, C. (2009). Do Duluth model interventions with perpetrators of domestic violence violate mental health professional ethics? *Ethics & Behavior, 19,* 323–340.

Dalton, B. (2009). Battered program directors' view on substance abuse and domestic violence. *Journal of Aggression, Maltreatment & Trauma, 18,* 248–260.

Featherstone, B., & Peckover, S. (2007). Letting them get away with it: Fathers, domestic violence and child welfare. *Critical Social Policy, 27,* 181–202.

Fenton, B., & Rathus, J. H. (2010). Men's self-reported descriptions and precipitants of domestic violence perpetration as reported in intake evaluations. *Journal of Family Violence, 25,* 149–158.

Fleck-Henderson, A., & Arean, J. C. (2004, July). *Breaking the cycle: Fathering after violence.* San Francisco: Family Violence Prevention Fund.

Francis, K., & Wolfe, D. (2008). Cognitive and emotional differences between abusive and non-abusive fathers. *Child Abuse & Neglect, 32,* 1127–1137.

Goetz, A., Shackelford, T., Romero, G., Kaighobadi, F., & Miner, E. (2008). Punishment, proprietariness, and paternity: Men's violence against women from an evolutionary perspective. *Aggression and Violent Behavior, 13,* 481–489.

Gondolf, E. W. (2007). Outcomes of case management for African-American men in batterer counseling. *Journal of Family Violence, 23,* 173–181.

Gondolf, E. W., & Williams, O. J. (2001). Culturally focused batterer counseling for African American men. *Trauma, Violence & Abuse, 2,* 283–295.

Hancock, T., & Siu, K. (2009). A culturally sensitive intervention with domestically violent Latino immigrant men. *Journal of Family Violence, 24,* 123–132.

Healey, K., Smith, C., & O'Sullivan, C. (1998, February). *Batterer's intervention: Program approaches and criminal justice strategies.* Washington, DC: U.S. Department of Justice, Office of Justice Programs.

Holtzworth-Munroe, A., Meehan, J. C., Herron, K., Rehman, U., & Stuart, G. L. (2003). Do subtypes of martially violent men continue to differ over time? *Journal of Consulting and Clinical Psychology, 71,* 728–740.

Holtzworth-Munroe, A., & Stuart, G. (1994). The relationship standards and assumptions of violent versus nonviolent husbands. *Cognitive Therapy & Research, 18,* 87–103

Huss, M. T., Covell, C. N., & Langhinrichsen-Rohling, J. (2006). Clinical implications for the assessment and treatment of antisocial and psychopathic domestic violence perpetrators. *Journal of Aggression, Maltreatment & Trauma, 13,* 59–85.

Jaffe, P., & Crooks, C. (2004). Partner violence and child custody cases. *Violence Against Women, 10,* 917–934.

Jaffe, P., Crooks, C., & Wolfe, D. (2003). Legal and policy responses to children exposed to domestic violence: The need to evaluate intended and unintended consequences. *Clinical Child and Family Psychology Review, 6,* 205–213.

Jakupcak, M., Lisak, D., & Roemer, L. (2002). The role of masculine ideology and masculine gender role stress in men's perpetration of relationship violence. *Psychology of Men & Masculinity, 3,* 97–106.

Little, L., & Kaufman Kantor, G. (2002). Using ecological theory to understand intimate partner violence and child maltreatment. *Journal of Community Health Nursing, 19,* 133–145.

Lohr, J., Bonge, D., Witte, T., Hamberger, K., & Langhinrichsen-Rohling, J. (2005). Consistency and accuracy of batterer typology identification. *Journal of Family Violence, 20,* 253–258.

Morrill, A., Jianyu, D., Dunn, S., Sung, I., & Smith, K. (2005). Child custody and visitation decisions when the father has perpetrated violence against the mother. *Violence Against Women, 11,* 1076–1107.

Oehme, K., & Maxwell, S. (2004). Florida's supervised visitation programs: The next phase. *Florida Bar Journal, 78,* 44–48.

Roberts, A. (2007). Domestic violence continuum, forensic assessment and crisis intervention. *Families in Society, 88,* 42–54.

Rothman, E., Butchart, A., & Cerda, M. (2003). *Intervening with perpetrators of intimate partner violence: A global perspective.* Geneva: World Health Organization.

Saez-Betacourt, A., Lam, B. T., & Nguyen, T. (2008). The meaning of being incarcerated on a domestic violence charge and its impact on self and family among Latino immigrant batterers. *Journal of Ethnic and Cultural Diversity in Social Work, 17,* 130–156.

Smith, E. (2008). African American men and intimate partner violence. *Journal of African American Studies, 12,* 156–179.

Stahly, G. (2007). Domestic violence and child custody: A critique of recent JCC articles. *Journal of Child Custody, 4,* 1–18.

Stanford, M. S., Houston, R. J., & Baldridge, R. M. (2008). Comparison of impulsive and premeditated perpetrators of intimate partner violence. *Behavioral Sciences & the Law, 26,* 709–722.

Stark, E. (2009). Rethinking custody evaluation in cases involving domestic violence. *Journal of Child Custody, 6,* 287–321.

Stern, N., & Oehme, K. (2007). Increasing safety for battered women and their children: Creating a privilege for supervised visitation intake records. *University of Richmond Law Review, 41,* 499–534.

Stoops, C., Bennett, L., & Vincent, N. (2010). Development and predictive ability of a behavior-based typology of men who batter. *Journal of Family Violence, 25,* 325–335.

Thomas, M., & Bennett, L. (2009). The co-occurrence of substance abuse and domestic violence: A comparison of dual-problem men in substance abuse treatment and in a court-ordered batterer program. *Journal of Social Work Practice in the Addictions, 9,* 299–317.

Tilley, D. S., & Brackley, M. (2005). Men who batter intimate partners: A grounded theory study of the development of male violence in intimate partner relationships. *Issues in Mental Health Nursing, 26,* 281–297.

Tilley, D. S., Rugari, S. M., & Walker, C. A. (2008). Development of violence in men who batter intimate partners: A case study. *Journal of Theory Construction & Testing, 12,* 28–33.

White, R., & Gondolf, E. (2000). Implications of personality profiles for batterer treatment. *Journal of Interpersonal Violence, 15,* 467–488.

Whitfield, C. L., Anda, R. F., Dube, S. R., & Felitti, V. J. (2003). Violent childhood experiences and the risk of intimate partner violence in adults: Assessment in a large health maintenance organization. *Journal of Interpersonal Violence, 18,* 166–185.

Williams, O. J. (2008). Healing and confronting the African American male who batters. In R. Carrillo & J. Tello (Eds.), *Family violence and men of color: Healing the wounded male spirit* (pp. 85–116). New York: Springer.

Williams, O. J., & Becker, L. (1994). Partner abuse programs and cultural competence: The results of a national study. *Violence and Victim, 9,* 287–295.

Williams, O. J., Oliver, W., & Pope, M. (2008). Domestic violence in the African American community. *Journal of Aggression, Maltreatment & Trauma, 16,* 229–237.

Zorza, J. (2009). On navigating custody and visitation evaluations in cases with domestic violence: A judge's guide. *Journal of Child Custody, 6,* 258–286.

Select Resources

- *Center for Family Policy and Practice:* http://www.cffpp.org/publications/fatherhood_programs.html

- *Center for Urban Families:* http://www.cfuf.org/index.php

- *Men Stopping Violence:* http://www.menstoppingviolence.org/

- *National Center for Fathering:* http://www.fathers.com/

- *National Institute of Justice:* http://www.ojp.usdoj.gov/nij/pubs-sum/195079.htm

- *StopFamilyViolence.org:* http://www.stopfamilyviolence.org/info/custody-abuse/overview/the-batterer-as-parent

- *VawNet:* http://new.vawnet.org/

Eight

State of Intimate Partner Violence Prevention, Intervention, and Research

In this chapter, I focus on the state of intimate partner violence prevention, intervention, and research. I explore the role of evidence-based practice as it relates to domestic violence as well as the challenges of conducting research in this area. Select prevention and intervention strategies are identified. I also examine the connection between research and practice and identify needed best practices in collaboration in the area of domestic violence.

When one examines intervention development, evidence-based practice, and domestic violence, it is important to first consider the historical context of the domestic violence movement. The civil rights and black liberation movement laid the groundwork for the feminist movement in the 1960s that brought voice to women's violent experiences in their own homes. The movement against domestic violence largely began with women coming together and organizing to shed light on this abuse, supporting women with safe alternatives, and preventing abuse of women through changes in policy and practice within communities and at multiple levels of government (Danis, 2003; Danis & Lockhart, 2003). The movement was radical and revolutionary and not rooted in the idea of science and research development but instead in helping women, advocating for change, and creating solutions to address both systemic and individual injustices. The field has grown to appreciate the importance of research, but with respect to how it can be used to advocate for social justice, safety, improved services, and equity. Too often, research and science are not rooted in principles of social justice and can continue to reinforce and perpetuate gender inequity (Colarossi, 2005). The importance of using research and science to advance the empowerment and social justice mandates of and by women is well supported among domestic violence advocates (Jordan, 2009). The evidence-based practice movement has further illustrated advocates' concerns with its emphasis on rigid definitions of what constitutes science. The story of one person is viewed as valid in the field, yet that same story is often considered inefficient and lacking rigor by the scientific community. The use of control groups has also come under scrutiny when a woman at risk is denied an intervention on the basis of a numeric formula that determines who should receive the service and who should be in the control group. Researchers who promote evidence-based practices have started to emphasize the importance of using different methodology, greater input from practitioners, and the idea that interventions can be adapted to diverse populations. The focus has also been on investigating practice-informed research, which emphasizes the importance of furthering practices in the field that work. Regardless, for some, the challenge remains to link science and research development with the movement's commitment to advancing social justice and empowering women. The scientific community has emphasized the need to create programs and services that have proven effectiveness and are developed on solid practices. The domestic violence community has emphasized the need to conduct research that is meaningful and useful to the population and that in and of itself is empowering and promotes the voice and experiences of diverse groups of women to keep them safe. In some ways, both communities serve to balance each other.

Interventions and programs are needed to meet the needs of diverse groups. What works for one group of people may not work for another because of different historical and life experiences, unequal distribution of resources, and persistent institutional and environmental discrimination. Projections are that by 2050 half of U.S. citizens will be people of color. Consequently, the need to determine best practices and identify programs that meet the needs of diverse populations is critical and timely. One of the major challenges practitioners face in the area of intervention research is that there continues to be a one-size-fits-all approach. As a result, services are less effective because the social determinants and context of the lives of the people practitioners serve are not recognized and accounted for. The idea of being colorblind is not only not working, but also can, in many cases, be harmful to the very people practitioners are trying to help. Research endeavors have to be framed with the idea of creating systems to meet the needs of people where they are as opposed to what is most convenient for the provider, community, and service system. Addressing these issues goes back to the very tenets of the domestic violence movement by recognizing the voices of others, empowering women to create change, coming to the population to find solutions, giving people the support they need to generate a movement that responds best to what they are experiencing, and not feeling as though formal structures have all the answers. It is critical that researchers approach intervention development and research from that stance as opposed to thinking that the answers rest within these formal systems.

Evidence-based Practice

Evidence-based practice "focuses on using intervention approaches with demonstrated effectiveness for a client's particular presenting problem or condition in collaboration with the client" (Adams, Matto, & LeCroy, 2009, p. 165). The role of evidence-based practice and social work has been considered in several substantive areas, such as substance abuse, mental health, and HIV interventions. Interventions in these areas have been tested and deemed to be evidence based; however, domestic violence has not necessarily been as quickly made a part of the evidence-based practice movement.

Proponents of evidence-based practice believe that using practices that have been tested leads to increases in

- the opportunity to provide more effective services

- the ability to be more accountable to stakeholders, such as clients, policymakers, and funders

- the opportunity to build on the science in the area

- the opportunity to create more options for intervening in domestic violence situations at the individual, community, and societal levels (Gambrill, 2007; Gibbs & Gambrill, 2002; Manuel, Mullen, Fang, Bellamy, & Bledsoe, 2009; Walker, Koroloff, Briggs, & Friesen, 2007)

Opponents of evidence-based practice have several concerns with the approach, asserting that

- many evidence-based programs lack generalizability to diverse groups because they have been tested with very limited populations

- the idea of what qualifies as evidence has been debated

- practitioners do not have the time to investigate evidence-based programs as they negotiate high caseloads and complex case issues in daily practice

- few evidence-based programs incorporate or acknowledge indigenous programs and interventions that have worked in communities

- the focus on evidence-based programs and practices has reduced funding and support to examine other indigenous or practice-based models

- the individual voices and experiences of women are not heard (Adams et al., 2009; Aisenberg, 2008; Gilbert, Harvey, & Belgrave, 2009; Gould, 2010; Maynard, 2010)

Although some resistance to using evidence-based practices in the field has been found, advocates, domestic violence providers, and law enforcement officers are increasingly using evidence-based practices to make decisions. For example, in various parts of the country the Danger Assessment (Campbell, 1986, 2007) is used in domestic violence and social services agencies, county law enforcement, and even health settings to assess danger and respond appropriately. Practitioners often use safety plans in the field, as opposed to generating them individually. The ability to research and adapt the use of a safety planning tool is a form of using an established practice for decision making. These actions point to the use of evidence to support decision making. As the field continues to grow, tools, strategies, models, and interventions will increasingly be used to further practices. I believe that these practices will still be rooted in advancing the cause of domestic violence beyond the science to include the advocacy agenda at the heart of the movement.

Prevention Strategies

The three levels of prevention are (1) primary prevention, which focuses on populations that have not experienced the issue; (2) secondary prevention, which focuses on people who are at great risk of experiencing the issue; and (3) tertiary prevention, which focuses on providing services for people who have been affected by the issue. In this section, I focus on primary prevention and the importance of addressing intimate partner violence before it occurs. So often money and time are spent working on interventions for people who have already experienced or perpetrated abuse. Although these interventions are critical, resources, time, and funding must also be provided for primary prevention, to help people avoid experiencing or perpetrating abuse.

Workplace Intervention

Policy interventions can be a form of primary prevention. They give practitioners an opportunity to generate procedures and rules to address the needs of populations before problems occur. Policy is not limited to macro-level policies but also encompasses agency and organizational policies, protocols, and procedures developed at the agency, school, or faith-based level. Practitioners ordinarily look at policy at the macro level rather than at the level of preventing issues from occurring within organizations and organizational structures. Policies and protocols can be developed to prevent violence in the workplace. Domestic violence is a workplace issue because of decreased productivity, worker safety, unplanned absences, and the tension that can be created in the work environment when someone is being abused. The survivor may be afraid to say anything out of embarrassment or fear of losing employment. Employers can create workplace policies that provide women with information about indicators of abuse, protocols on how to respond to abuse, and procedures to ensure their safety. These protocols could include

- providing training to all employees on the definition and cycle of domestic violence as a standard and ongoing practice

- having referral information available on safety planning, counseling, and the location of emergency services

- posting information about domestic violence and where to go for help in bathroom stalls

- outlining the workplace's response to domestic violence, which could include job transfers, changed schedules, identification of an emergency contact person, or having a code word for when one is in danger

- working with advocates to offer training on domestic violence in the workplace

- developing specific ways to maintain safety in the workplace

- helping to identify ways of communicating safety concerns without blaming the survivor

- displaying policies, procedures, and protocols so that employees understand the employer's commitment to this issue.

Faith-based Intervention

Faith-based communities play a major role in this issue and can be better engaged in supporting primary prevention efforts. Anyone concerned about the life of the church and people's spiritual growth should be committed to addressing intimate partner violence. People who attend faith-based communities have been found to be at risk for experiencing violence (Bent-Goodley, 2006; Brade & Bent-Goodley, 2009; Manetta, Bryant, Cavanaugh, & Gange, 2003). Some faith-based organizations have condoned the violence by using sacred scripture and emphasizing the sanctity of marriage at all costs. Women are often given messages that exacerbate their risk. For example, they are told that

- marriage is a private issue, meaning that they should not seek outside support
- they should forgive, meaning that they are responsible for maintaining the relationship and overlooking the violence
- they should not air dirty laundry, meaning that they should suffer in silence.

Those most concerned about strengthening faith-based communities should also be concerned about intimate partner violence. Most denominations have a formal position on domestic violence and have affirmed that the religious community does not condone, and in fact stands against, domestic violence (Bent-Goodley & Fowler, 2006; Fortune, 2006). However, all too often local faith-based groups do not know that their denomination has a policy statement on domestic violence. It is important that the different denominations know, understand, and support their policy statements as a form of primary prevention. Some specific things that faith-based communities can do to evidence their commitment to stopping domestic violence are to

- provide sermons that speak against domestic violence
- create a safe place to talk about domestic violence
- provide healthy relationship education
- lead by example; model fairness and equity regardless of gender throughout the church and in how it functions
- identify theology and scripture that reinforce domestic violence prevention
- partner with local providers to share community resources
- obtain and support training on domestic violence so that the congregation has trained people who can help

- not provide pastoral counseling in this area if they are not equipped to do so

- provide information about domestic violence in bathroom stalls and key locations in the church

- partner with a local provider to conduct domestic violence education and awareness for people preparing for marriage.

Community-based Intervention

Community-based organizations can also engage in primary prevention in the natural environment and encourage communities to generate and develop ways of responding to issues not just in faith-based communities but also in grassroots organizations, fraternities, sororities, and civic organizations. These local groups can provide mutual aid and informal support around this issue and mentor young people, emphasizing healthy relationships. They can provide forums, training, and other events that promote healthy relationships and dating violence prevention education. These organizations can be powerful allies and hold formal provider systems accountable for the services provided in the community. They can work with providers to craft culturally specific messages promoting prevention in their communities. The field talks a lot about developing coordinated community responses. Yet, these groups are often composed of people in a fragmented formal provider network, not of people from the informal community network (Klevens, Baker, Shelley, & Ingram, 2008; Pennington-Zoellner, 2009). It is imperative that these informal, grassroots organizations not only be included, but also have equal voice in decision making on how to best promote programs within the community. These groups can also use their unique role in terms of individual and community empowerment and provide support to people who value that particular message by organizing events and promoting health and wellness. Again, these groups have a unique opportunity to become more responsive so that they are not only included but encouraged and supported in assuming leadership in designing prevention methods and strategies. Community groups can do the following to engage in domestic violence prevention:

- Host events on domestic violence prevention and healthy relationship education.

- Support and partner with a local domestic violence provider to make donations to the program or conduct education efforts together.

- Have referral information available at community events.

- Lead by example; model gender equity regardless of organizational membership.

- Promote equality in gender relationships.

- Obtain training in domestic violence so that members can serve as an informed resource.

- Participate in local domestic violence organizations to provide a community perspective on domestic violence.

- Advocate for policies that keep victims safe in the local community.

- Develop mentoring, after-school, or camp programs for children and youths, targeting domestic violence and dating violence prevention.

- Conduct manhood and fatherhood programs that promote being violence free and having healthy relationships in the community.

Schools and Domestic Violence Prevention

Schools are critical partners for change. They house students for six to 10 hours each day and provide opportunities for socialization and discussion of healthy relationships, the identification of abuse, and the ability to provide support and treatment during early stages of relationship development. In addition, because youths are already in the building, schools allow for the advancement of an important conversation regarding dating violence and domestic violence in a familiar location. Some local governments require that dating violence prevention education be provided in local school districts. Some specific activities that schools can engage in are to

- provide dating violence education as part of a developmentally age-appropriate curriculum that also includes co-occurring issues such as cyberbullying, bullying, stalking, and sexual harassment

- provide healthy relationship education
- create locations within the school where students can get information about dating violence prevention
- put posters and other information on dating violence and domestic violence awareness and prevention education in key locations
- develop a relationship with providers to make referrals
- solicit children's ideas on how to respond to domestic violence in the home as witnesses and how to respond to dating violence
- make referrals to providers
- model the behavior being sought from the young people on violence prevention and gender equity
- train personnel on dating violence and domestic violence on an ongoing basis
- identify and connect with counseling resources for child witnesses of domestic violence and youths who are in or aware of someone in a dating violence situation.
- know the laws of your local community in relation to dating violence
- partner with community-based organizations and groups to host events and other programs related to domestic violence and dating violence.

Men and Boys Supporting Prevention

Bringing men and boys to the table to promote prevention is also critical. For many years, the focus on organizing has understandably centered on bringing women together to resolve this issue. It is vitally important to ensure that women's voices stay at the center of the issue. However, it is also important to recognize that domestic violence is not just a woman's issue. Intimate partner violence affects men and boys, communities, and the larger society, and so the answer and the resolution do not rest solely in the hands of women. Ensuring that men and boys are a part of this prevention movement and that their voices are heard allows the development and design of more effective prevention messages (Crooks, Goodall, Hughes, Jaffe, & Baker, 2007). Through gender-specific programs and prevention interventions that promote nonviolence in relationships and through healthy relationship education, primary prevention efforts can use developmentally age-appropriate strategies to advance understanding of domestic violence prevention in communities. More prevention messages that are specific and singularly focused on engaging men in preventing violence are needed. These primary prevention efforts can also target promoting gender equity and flexible gender-role perceptions to address the societal and environmental context in which intimate partner violence takes place. Thus, as practitioners talk about health and wellness in intimate relationships, they can also promote healthy and equitable gender relationships across organizations and communities. These organizational and structural changes by leaders can translate into health and wellness in individual relationships and more. Men and boys can be engaged to

- participate in prevention education efforts
- become more aware of how to respond to domestic violence
- speak out against domestic violence in individual, family, community, organizational, and faith-based settings
- engage in manhood and fatherhood training that supports healthy relationships
- reinforce the importance of healthy, nonviolent relationships in discussion with boys and girls
- obtain additional training to be informed helpers.

Community and Public Education Strategies

Community and public education are critical to supporting primary prevention efforts. These community and public education strategies must use creative, culturally proficient and developmentally appropriate messaging that promotes healthy relationships and the idea that these relationships can exist and that inform communities about domestic violence indicators and strategies to prevent violence. Public education and community awareness must be considered in terms of product and location. The product should focus on what the messaging looks like. It must provide information and education and encourage the person to want to learn more. The message should set the tone that intimate partner violence is wrong, that domestic violence is not an individual issue, and that resources and services are available in communities that can help to respond to this issue. At the same time, location must be considered because even if the messaging is powerful, it will not be effective if it is not reaching people. When considering location, think about where people go and where they might be most willing to listen to and talk about these issues. For example, the barbershop and beauty salon may be excellent locations, particularly in communities of color where people are already engaged in these kinds of discussions and where a natural system of communication and support is in place. Sports, after-school, and music programs are great natural environments in which to engage in outreach with young people who may not access formal services but are in need of assistance. Social media networks also provide opportunities to provide messaging. For example, Facebook, Twitter, blogs, and other social networking can expand access to information and provide a forum in which to exchange information and get support. Text messaging, for example, could be used during targeted periods, such as during the Super Bowl or holidays, when domestic violence increases, to provide public education messages at critical time points. Public education must be centered on

- culturally and developmentally specific messaging
- reaching wider audiences and diverse populations
- promoting what is available in the local community to enhance awareness of resources
- setting a tone that does not condone abuse
- discussing and identifying what a healthy relationship looks like
- targeting critical time periods in which the risk of violence increases and enhancing messaging during that time
- using social networks as a violence prevention tool.

Interventions

Interventions are increasingly being developed to address domestic violence. Certainly, the most familiar interventions are policy-based interventions, shelter-based interventions, and criminal justice policy and program interventions. Although these interventions are important, it is also important to acknowledge emerging interventions and needs that require attention.

Public Policy as Intervention

Public policy is a critical form of intervention. Several national-level policies have shaped and supported intervention on domestic violence. The Family Violence Prevention and Services Act (FVPSA) was first enacted in 1984 as part of Title III of the Child Abuse Amendment. It provides the largest source of funding for emergency services in the area of domestic violence. FVPSA funds emergency shelter programs and services for survivors of domestic violence and their children. It also targets the development of programs and services for culturally and linguistically diverse populations. FVPSA is a critical policy that funds programs and interventions on the ground each day. It is a safety net for domestic violence programming that supports services at the state, tribal, and local levels, including funding national resource centers, state coalitions, hotlines, and more than 2,000 shelter programs and safe houses across the country. It strengthens collaborative interdisciplinary networks related to domestic violence and enhances direct legal and housing assistance.

The Violence Against Women Act (VAWA) (P.L. 103-322) was first passed in 1994 and then reauthorized in 2000 and 2005. VAWA reinforced the federal role in domestic violence prevention and expanded the government's response to domestic violence to include legal sanctions for abuse, greater involvement and support for the law enforcement response to domestic violence, increased service options for domestic violence survivors, and support for particularly challenged populations, such as the immigrant community, people with disabilities, and culturally diverse groups. Each reauthorization has focused on an enhancement of the population affected and greater recognition of the wide-reaching impact and needed response to domestic violence.

Overview of VAWA Provisions

Law Enforcement

- increased collaboration among law enforcement, domestic violence, and social service organizations
- provided interstate protections through enforcement of protection orders across states
- made domestic violence prosecutable across state lines
- created and supports mandatory arrest laws
- incorporated and strengthened laws for stalking, sexual assault, and dating violence to help local communities more readily address this crime
- supported community-coordinated responses to encourage interdisciplinary collaboration and enhanced responses

Underserved Populations

- supported enhanced cultural and linguistic services among diverse populations
- increased supports for teenagers and people with disabilities
- enhanced clarity of and created laws to support immigrants experiencing domestic violence

Service Provision

- increased legal assistance for victims' services
- provided funding for primary prevention activities
- increased housing options and created laws to prevent domestic violence–related evictions for survivors
- promoted and supports supervised visitation models

The Family Violence Option (FVO) is a program offered through Temporary Assistance for Needy Families. It allows public service workers to make work and time requirement exceptions for people who have experienced domestic violence. Most states have a FVO provision, although it is not required at this time. States that support this provision screen for domestic violence and can then offer or require that the person receive domestic violence counseling and assistance as part of his or her public benefits. Although the program has been effective, some concerns with its implementation exist. For example, the conditions for granting waivers, referral processes and client monitoring, the process of conducting the screenings, insufficient training of staff and awareness of domestic violence, and requirements for domestic violence survivors to be in treatment differ from state to state (Casey, Davies, Gifford, & Menard, 2010; General Accounting Office, 2005; Payne & Triplett, 2009).

These policies provide federal leadership on the issue of domestic violence, dating violence, sexual assault, and stalking that is critical to advance the discourse on these issues at the state and local levels. Although they are important, much is still required at the state and local levels to advance gun laws that make sense, ensure the implementation of these policies to enhance services to survivors, and provide greater resources and policy development to address the local population's unique needs and factors. Reauthorization of the FVPSA and VAWA should be an ongoing effort, and widening the FVO to all states with greater monitoring of its implementation is a necessary focus for advocacy in the future.

Shelters

Certainly, shelter-based programs continue to be critical to serving women affected by domestic violence. Shelters provide women with a safe place to live, crisis intervention, housing, emergency services, counseling and mental health services for themselves and their children, and legal services. Shelters have expanded their services to meet the needs of women and children seeking services. They provide a short-term solution while women develop long-term strategies and safety plans leading to their independence in a supportive and safe environment. The first shelter was opened in 1974 in St. Paul, Minnesota. Women's advocates continue to provide important services to women today, along with a minimum of 2,000 shelters and safe houses across the country. Although shelters are not the only intervention service available, they continue to be critical, and their role and function in aiding women cannot be diminished.

Shelters are, however, being asked to respond to women with multiple, increasingly complicated needs. They are challenged with serving more women than they have beds for. In addition, they are faced with responding to the unique needs of diverse groups, immigration issues, and co-occurring issues such as HIV and substance abuse. Teenagers are also increasingly seeking shelter services. One should not assume that young people have housing or are living in homes with parents who can keep them safe. Some young people are living in foster care, group homes, or independent living settings. Consequently, shelters are responding to the needs of different populations with different specific demands and requirements, all in need of shelter and safety in crisis situations. The landscape is becoming increasingly more complicated, with fewer and fewer resources. Many shelters struggle just to keep up with the needs of women, and they are always challenged by having to turn women and children away because of limited resources and lack of beds. This necessity is unconscionable when its impact on people and communities is considered.

Criminal Justice Policies and Programs

Criminal justice programs have received increasing attention as a result of VAWA's substantiating law enforcement's and the legal system's role in responding to domestic violence. In addition to local police departments' developing specialized domestic violence units within the police department (Bledsoe, Sar, & Barbee, 2006), law enforcement has also responded through mandatory arrest laws, and the use of protection orders and domestic violence courts has received considerable attention in the criminal justice arena.

Mandatory Arrest Policy

Mandatory arrest policy is another effective tool used to address domestic violence. The policy and its use varies across states. Twenty states and the District of Columbia have a mandatory arrest policy, 21 states have a policy that arrest is at the discretion of the officer, and nine states have a proarrest policy that does not require an arrest but supports the use of arrest as a response to domestic violence (American Bar Association, 2007; RADAR, 2008).

Table 8-1: Overview of States Laws Related to Mandatory Arrest Policy

Officer's Discretion	Proarrest	Mandatory Arrest
Alabama	Arkansas	Alaska
Delaware	California	Arizona
Georgia	Florida	Colorado
Hawaii	Massachusetts	Connecticut
Idaho	Michigan	District of Columbia
Illinois	Montana	Iowa
Indiana	North Dakota	Kansas
Kentucky	Tennessee	Louisiana
Maryland	Wisconsin	Maine
Minnesota		Mississippi
Missouri		Nevada
Nebraska		New Jersey
New Hampshire		New York
New Mexico		Ohio
North Carolina		Oregon
Oklahoma		Rhode Island
Pennsylvania		South Carolina
Texas		South Dakota
Vermont		Utah
West Virginia		Virginia
Wyoming		Washington

Source: Adapted from the American Bar Association Commission on Domestic Violence (http://new.abanet.org/domesticviolence/Pages/default.aspx)

According to the National Incident Based Reporting System, mandatory arrest policies have resulted in an increase in arrest patterns for domestic violence (Hirschel, Buzawa, Pattavina, & Faggiani, 2007). Police are making four times more arrests for domestic violence than in the 1970s and 1980s (Hirschel et al., 2007). A mandatory arrest policy reduces police discretion in making an arrest for domestic violence. The police officer cannot take into account the survivor's recommendation to arrest or not arrest the perpetrator (Phillips & Sobol, 2010). However, the police officer does have some discretion in determining who is the primary aggressor in the situation. Mandatory arrests are more likely to take place if there is a visible injury, when there is a protection order, or when the perceived perpetrator is disrespectful to the police officer (Phillips & Sobol, 2010). The number of dual arrests, in which survivors are also being arrested, is also increasing (Hirschel et al., 2007). This measure is taken to allow the criminal justice system to prosecute people for domestic violence, recognizing that victims often retract their statement out of fear of the perpetrator, because of pressure from family and friends, or because of the notion that the violence will stop (Ford & Breall, 2000). Mandatory arrest policy allows cases to be brought against perpetrators without the victim's support. Proponents of mandatory arrest policy state that it holds perpetrators more accountable, it relieves the woman from having to justify her actions to the perpetrator because the system is bringing the charge as opposed to the woman, and it can prevent future violence toward the woman and perhaps toward other women. Opponents of mandatory arrest policy state that taking the choice away from the survivor adds to the woman's feelings of powerlessness and that the system takes the perpetrator's place by using power and control to usurp the woman's decision-making authority. The other issue related to mandatory arrest policy is that it is at times difficult to determine who is the primary aggressor, and in those situations dual arrest is more likely to take place. As a result, the survivor is also arrested. Dual arrests often occur when officers have had inadequate training or cannot determine who is the primary aggressor (O'Dell, 2007). Dual arrest is one unintended consequence of the mandatory arrest policy, along with unwanted arrests when the survivor is uncomfortable or feels at greater risk because of the arrest and retaliatory arrests in which the perpetrator encourages dual arrest by using the policy to create doubt as to who is the primary aggressor (Frye, Haviland, & Rajah, 2007; Hirschel et al., 2007). These unintended consequences have reinforced the need for risk assessment and management tools that are more comprehensive and that include lethality assessment as part of the mandatory arrest process (Hoyle, 2008; White, Goldkamp, & Campbell, 2005). Mandatory arrest processes need to include practices that identify high-risk situations, make referrals as part of safety planning, and conduct lethality assessments to ensure that follow-up takes place in high-risk situations.

Protection Orders

People often seek civil protection orders for emotional and psychological abuse and criminal protection orders for physical violence (Kethineni & Beichner, 2009). Twenty percent of survivors obtain civil protection orders (Tjaden & Thoennes, 2000), which do result in a decline in abuse. One study found that abuse declined from 68 percent to 23 percent after the survivor obtained a protection order (Carlson, Harris, & Holden, 1999). Despite claims that protection orders do not work, overall women with a protection order experience reduced violence, less severe violence, and a longer time between violent episodes (Ford & Breall, 2000). These experiences are typically the same regardless of marital status (Shannon, Logan, & Cole, 2007). Particularly violent people or ex-partners do pose additional risks for violence regardless of the order (Logan, Shannon, Walker, & Faragher, 2006). Unfortunately, although judges are able to remove firearms when protection orders are granted, they often do not inform the survivor of this opportunity or use the provision in their decision-making process (Webster et al., 2010). Additional points to share with survivors about protection orders are as follows;

- Protection orders can be effective, but it is important for the survivor to consistently enforce the order. It is most effective when followed and used.

- Protection orders should be given along with a lethality assessment. If the level of lethality is high, then the protection order should be coupled with additional safety planning efforts to better support the survivor's safety.

- Protection orders provide a paper trail. They provide the survivor with a documented account of the violence that has been experienced. This documentation can be important in the event the perpetrator attempts to build a false case against the survivor.

- The protection order can also be helpful in documenting a need for public welfare benefits, immigration, and other public services.

- If lethality does occur, the protection order provides specific information for the family members, attorney, and fatality review committee members to track the violence and create systems improvements for future survivors.

Consequently, protection orders are not futile. They are an important tool in responding to domestic violence. Protection orders can be very effective with perpetrators who may be afraid of law enforcement, have employment to lose, or fear losing status in the neighborhood or place of employment. Protection orders are often less effective with perpetrators who have nothing to lose, do not fear law enforcement responses, or are unemployed. These issues are critical to understand and connect to lethality reviews, safety planning, and enhancing community supports that reinforce the importance of protection orders.

Domestic Violence Courts

Domestic violence courts are important court-based domestic violence interventions that are achieving increased momentum in the legal system. These specialized courts are centered around three particular areas: (1) increasing the safety of the survivor and children, (2) holding the perpetrator accountable, and (3) reducing future violence. Over the past 10 years, the number of domestic violence courts has grown from 42 to 208 (Labriola, Bradley, O'Sullivan, Rempel, & Moore, 2010). They can be found in 32 states, with the highest concentration in California and New York. Domestic violence courts have been found to be successful in encouraging a more active and informed role for judges, expanded services for survivors, increased use of court monitoring of perpetrators, more consistent response, better coordination of services, and more dedicated processing of domestic violence cases (Eley, 2005; Gover, Brank, & MacDonald, 2007; Gover, MacDonald, & Alpert, 2003; Mirchandani, 2004, 2005). Having these specialized courts also encourages greater collaboration among referral sources and partners working on domestic violence issues and can thus affect systems that touch survivors' lives. The participation of these community and service-related entities is critical to the success of the domestic violence court model.

Child Welfare Interventions

In the child welfare system, tools and interventions are increasingly being used to better respond to domestic violence. Child welfare interventions are going beyond immediately removing the child because he or she has witnessed violence and incorporating other strategies to respond. Two emerging interventions receiving increased attention are family team conferencing and early childhood interventions.

Family Team Conferencing

Family team conferencing is a tool currently being used in the child welfare system and examined in the response to domestic violence. *Family team conferencing* has been defined as "a gathering of family members, friends, community specialists, and other interested people who join together to strengthen [the] family and provide a protection and care plan for the children" (Carter, 2003, p. 4). Using this intervention, an expert facilitator brings together the survivor, perpetrator, domestic violence advocates, batterers intervention staff, extended family, practitioners, and relevant faith-based and community partners to determine what is in the child's best interests, develop a plan that best serves the child, and build on decision making that furthers the child's safety and well-being. Proponents of using family team conferencing in domestic violence cases have identified the increase in developing solutions that keep children safe and the acknowledgment that perpetrators often continue to be involved in the lives of their children. This model provides a way to monitor and regulate the relationship. In addition, services are better integrated and coordinated across disciplines to ensure seamless and comprehensive care. The model also includes a focus on developing accountability measures. Community involvement allows the community to hold service providers accountable for needed care and to provide improved support to the family by knowing who to contact if a need emerges. Family team conferencing is emerging as an intervention strategy in the child welfare area and continues to be tested to determine its effectiveness and most appropriate use.

Early Childhood Interventions

The Office of Juvenile Justice and Delinquency Prevention is currently funding 15 promising programs that provide integrated services for children who have been exposed to domestic violence. These interventions build on the local community's cultural and geographic strengths and service delivery structure. Each of these programs is working on several critical areas and is locally driven, with the following foci:

- building programs' community capacity to address the needs of children exposed to domestic violence

- addressing the psychological issues children evidence after being exposed to domestic violence

- providing parents with case management services that include home visits

- conducting screenings to determine when domestic violence is occurring

- providing parenting education and health-based interventions for families

- providing education to teachers to ensure that they understand these issues

- using motivational interviewing to support interventions with children exposed to domestic violence

Challenges of Conducting Domestic Violence Research

The challenges of conducting domestic violence research are important to discuss. Conducting domestic violence research is crucial to advancing interventions that ensure that current programs and services are effective. A major issue that domestic violence researchers must consider is the ethical obligations of conducting research in this area. Safety must be a primary concern. Needed protocols must be put in place to ensure that being involved in the research does not pose undue risks and that there are benefits to the person participating. Examples of such protocols include the following:

- the perpetrator's showing up at a site and controlling the survivor's responses

- the perpetrator's finding materials from the intervention

- the lack of an available safety plan for the survivor

- the survivor's being traumatized by the research

- the perpetrator's attempting to harm the woman for participating
- the risk of putting others in danger from a perpetrator
- broken confidentiality
- the requirement for mandated reporting
- coercion to participate in the study

For these reasons, researchers must ensure that they have thought about these concerns and have protocols in place to respond should any issue arise. Referral sources should be available and agreed on before the research begins. Safety measures and safety principles must be developed at the very beginning of the process to reduce risks of participation. Levels of risk can be identified.

An additional ethical obligation in conducting domestic violence research is to ensure that the research meets the needs of diverse populations. Using a one-size-fits-all approach to domestic violence research is insufficient. Researchers should be required to recognize and plan for the unique challenges that could face diverse groups.

Researchers, domestic violence advocates and practitioners, and survivors must work together to develop interventions that make sense for the client. The scientific community must recognize that domestic violence is not just a research area but an opportunity to engage in empowerment research that is part of a larger movement. As a result, research needs to, on some level, speak to that history. Practitioners must also understand the nature of science development and work in collaboration with researchers to meet scientific obligations while supporting women and children. Practitioners must be empowered to inform what the research looks like and have a true partnership and collaboration in the research project. The focus must be on developing trust over time. Researchers need to be better engaged with domestic violence survivors and the community so they understand the dynamics and issues that occur. Community members should be acknowledged as experts and collaborators in addressing the issue. How domestic violence is measured also warrants greater attention. The measures and tools practitioners use often do not capture what they are meant to. Assessment tools have been developed to guide what practitioners know (Thompson, Basile, Hertz, & Sitterle, 2006). As their use is better coordinated across domestic violence research, researchers must also refine, test, and create new measures.

Reflecting Pool

In this chapter, I focused on research and intervention strategies in domestic violence. I should acknowledge that the field has progressed. Through more targeted laws and improved enforcement of current laws, development of critical interventions, and the continued evolution of best practices in the field, social workers continue to advance their understanding and create tools that can be used in the field. Although much has been accomplished, considerable work still lies ahead. The groundwork and foundation is strong but needs the commitment of future generations to advance the vision.

My Reflection

As a practitioner, I have been very invested in finding solutions to domestic violence, searching for best practices and answers to help the women, children, and men. I used research as a mechanism to find answers and solutions to the questions that most perplexed me. My research has always been grounded in a desire to respond to that one client, that one community, and that one population. Each question stems from a desire to create equity in situations of inequity and neglect. Research has always been a tool to advance the issue and to engender safety, well-being, and development among the people I serve. My commitment to this issue has shaped my work as a scholar, as a practitioner, as a woman, and as an African American woman committed to seeing the reduction in and eventual eradication of domestic violence. I have also been told that building working relationships between researchers and advocates is difficult. I feel that because I have always seen myself as both, I have never had difficulty engaging and working with the advocacy community. They have seen my commitment in my volunteering to serve on boards, conduct workshops and presentations, organize conferences, advocate at the local and national levels, use my research to advance the discourse, and even working directly with women, children, and teenagers. Witnessing my commitment has allowed the community of advocates and providers to see my authenticity. I view myself as creating a bridge between the two worlds. I believe that to do this work, one has to be driven by a commitment greater than the research question and centered on eliminating the need to ask it. I challenge the field to center itself on that discourse and continue to move the profession farther along.

Your Reflection

- What is your level of readiness to conduct this work?
- Do you have sufficient knowledge and skill to conduct domestic violence research?
- What is your level of investment in finding solutions to address domestic violence?
- Are you prepared to engage diverse populations in your research, and have you taken their needs into account?
- To what extent is the population a part of your research team, study design, and evaluation?

Notes:

_____

_____

_____

_____

_____

_____

_____

_____

_____

_____

_____

_____

References

Adams, K. B., Matto, H. C., & LeCroy, C. W. (2009). Limitations of evidence-based practice for social work education: Unpacking the complexity. *Journal of Social Work Education, 45,* 165–186.

Aisenberg, E. (2008). Evidence-based practice in mental health care to ethnic minority communities: Has its practice fallen short of its evidence? *Social Work, 53,* 297–306.

American Bar Association. (2007). *Commission on domestic violence.* Retrieved from http://new.abanet.org/domesticviolence/Pages/default.aspx

Bent-Goodley, T. B. (2006). Domestic violence and the black church: Challenging abuse one soul at a time. In R. L. Hampton & T. P. Gullotta (Eds.), *Interpersonal violence in the African-American community: Evidence-based prevention and treatment practices* (pp. 107–119). New York: Springer.

Bent-Goodley, T. B., & Fowler, D. N. (2006). Spiritual and religious abuse: Expanding what is known about domestic violence. *Affilia: Journal of Women and Social Work, 21,* 282–295.

Bledsoe, L., Sar, B., & Barbee, A. (2006). Impact of coordinated response to intimate partner violence on offender accountability. *Journal of Aggression, Maltreatment & Trauma, 13,* 109–129.

Brade, K., & Bent-Goodley, T. B. (2009). A refuge for my soul: Examining African American clergy's perceptions related to domestic violence awareness and engagement in faith community initiatives. *Social Work & Christianity, 36,* 430–448.

Campbell, J. C. (1986). Nursing assessment for risk of homicide with battered women. *Advances in Nursing Science, 8,* 36–51.

Campbell, J. C. (2007). *Assessing dangerousness.* New York: Springer.

Carlson, M., Harris, S., & Holden, G. (1999). Protective orders and domestic violence: Risk factors for re-abuse. *Journal of Family Violence, 14,* 205–226.

Carter, L. (2003). *Family team conferences in domestic violence cases: Guidelines for practices* (2nd ed.). San Francisco: Family Violence Prevention Fund.

Casey, T., Davies, J., Gifford, A., & Menard, A. (2010). *Not enough: What TANF offers family violence victims.* Harrisburg, PA: National Resource Center on Domestic Violence.

Colarossi, L. (2005). A response to Danis & Lockhart: What guides social work knowledge about violence against women? *Journal of Social Work Education, 41,* 147–159.

Crooks, C. V., Goodall, G. R., Hughes, R., Jaffe, P. G., & Baker, L. L. (2007). Engaging men and boys in preventing violence against women. *Violence Against Women, 13,* 217–239.

Danis, F. S. (2003). The criminalization of domestic violence: What social workers need to know. *Social Work, 48,* 237–246.

Danis, F., & Lockhart, L. (2003). Domestic violence and social work education: What do we know, what do we need to know? *Journal of Social Work Education, 39,* 215–225.

Eley, S. (2005). Changing practices: The specialized domestic violence court process. *Howard Journal of Criminal Justice, 44,* 113–124.

Ford, D. A., & Breall, S. (2000). *Violence against women: Synthesis of research for prosecutors* (NCJ 199660). Washington, DC: National Institute of Justice.

Fortune, M. M. (2006). National declaration of religious and spiritual leaders addressing violence against women. *Journal of Religion & Abuse, 8,* 71–77.

Frye, V., Haviland, M., & Rajah, V. (2007). Dual arrest and other unintended consequences of mandatory arrest in New York City: A brief report. *Journal of Family Violence, 22,* 397–405.

Gambrill, E. (2007). Views of evidence-based practice: Social workers' code of ethics and accreditation standards as guides for choice. *Journal of Social Work Education, 43,* 447–462.

General Accounting Office. (2005). *TANF: State approaches to screening for domestic violence could benefit from HHS guidance* (GAO-05-701). Washington, DC: Author.

Gibbs, L., & Gambrill, E. (2002). Evidence-based practice: Counterarguments to objections. *Research on Social Work Practice, 12,* 452–476.

Gilbert, D. J., Harvey, A. R., & Belgrave, F. Z. (2009). Advancing the Africentric paradigm shift discourse: Building toward evidence-based Africentric interventions in social work practice with African Americans. *Social Work, 54,* 243–252.

Gould, N. (2010). Integrating qualitative evidence in practice guideline development: Meeting the challenge of evidence-based practice for social work. *Qualitative Social Work, 9,* 93–109.

Gover, A. R., Brank, E. M., & MacDonald, J. M. (2007). A specialized domestic violence court in South Carolina. *Violence Against Women, 13,* 603–626.

Gover, A. R., MacDonald, J., & Alpert, G. (2003). Combating domestic violence: Findings from an evaluation of a local domestic violence court. *Criminology & Public Policy, 3,* 109–132.

Hirschel, D., Buzawa, E., Pattavina, A., & Faggiani, D. (2007). Domestic violence and mandatory arrest laws: To what extent do they influence police arrest decisions? *Journal of Criminal Law & Criminology, 98,* 255–298.

Hoyle, C. (2008). Will she be safe? A critical analysis of risk assessment in domestic violence cases. *Children & Youth Services Review, 30,* 323–337.

Jordan, C. (2009). Advancing the study of violence against women: Response to commentaries and next steps. *Violence Against Women, 15,* 440–442.

Keeping Children and Families Safe Act of 2003 (S. 345 and H.R. 14). (2003, March 5). [Government Relations Update]. Retrieved from http://www.naswdc.org/advocacy/updates/2003/030503.asp

Kethineni, S., & Beichner, D. (2009). A comparison of civil and criminal orders of protection as remedies for domestic violence victims in a Midwestern county. *Journal of Family Violence, 24,* 311–321.

Klevens, J., Baker, C., Shelley, G., & Ingram, E. (2008). Exploring the links between components of coordinated community responses and their impact on contact with intimate partner violence services. *Violence Against Women, 14,* 346–358.

Labriola, M., Bradley, S., O'Sullivan, C. S., Rempel, M., & Moore, S. (2010). *A national portrait of domestic violence courts.* Washington, DC: National Institute of Justice.

Logan, T. K., Shannon, L., Walker, R., & Faragher, T. M. (2006). Protective orders: Questions and conundrums. *Trauma, Violence & Abuse, 7,* 175–205.

Manetta, A. A., Bryant, D. F., Cavanaugh, T., & Gange, T. A. (2003). The church: Does it provide support for abused women? Differences in the perceptions of battered women and parishioners. *Journal of Religion & Abuse, 5,* 5–21.

Manuel, J. I., Mullen, E. J., Fang, L., Bellamy, J. L., & Bledsoe, S. E. (2009). Preparing social work practitioners to use evidence-based practice: A comparison of experiences from an implementation project. *Research on Social Work Practice, 19,* 613–627.

Maynard, B. R. (2010). Social service organizations in the era of evidence-based practice. *Journal of Social Work, 10,* 301–316.

Mirchandani, R. (2004). Battered women's movement ideals and judge-led social change in domestic violence courts. *Good Society Journal, 13,* 32–37.

Mirchandani, R. (2005). What's so special about specialized courts? The state and social change in Salt Lake City's Domestic Violence Court. *Law & Society Review, 39,* 379–418.

O'Dell, A. (2007). Why do police arrest victims of domestic violence? The need for comprehensive training and investigative protocols. *Journal of Aggression, Maltreatment & Trauma, 15,* 53–73.

Payne, B., & Triplett, R. (2009). Assessing the domestic violence training needs of benefits workers. *Journal of Family Violence, 24,* 243–253.

Pennington-Zoellner, K. (2009). Expanding "community" in the community response to intimate partner violence. *Journal of Family Violence, 24,* 539–545.

Phillips, S., & Sobol, J. (2010). Twenty years of mandatory arrest: Police decision making in the face of legal requirements. *Criminal Justice Policy Review, 21,* 98–118.

Respecting Accuracy in Domestic Abuse Reporting (RADAR). (2008). *An epidemic of civil rights abuses: Ranking of states' domestic violence laws.* Westfield, NJ: Author.

Shannon, L., Logan, T. K., & Cole, J. (2007). Intimate partner violence, relationship status, and protective orders. *Journal of Interpersonal Violence, 22,* 1114–1130.

Thompson, M., Basile, K., Hertz, M., & Sitterle, D. (2006). *Measuring intimate partner violence victimizaton and perpetration: A compendium of assessment tools.* Atlanta: Centers for Disease Control and Prevention.

Tjaden, P., & Thoennes, N. (2000). *Extent, nature and consequences of violence against women: Findings from the National Violence against Women Survey* (NCJ 181867). Washington, DC: Bureau of Justice Statistics.

Violence Against Women Act of 1994, P.L. 103-322, Title IV, 108, Stat. 1902.

Walker, J. S., Koroloff, N., Briggs, H. E., & Friesen, B. J. (2007). Implementing and sustaining evidence-based practice in social work. *Journal of Social Work Education, 43,* 361–375.

Webster, D., Frattaroli, S., Vernick, J., O'Sullivan, C., Roehl, J., & Campbell, J. (2010). Women with protective orders report failure to remove firearms from their abusive partners: Results from an exploratory study. *Journal of Women's Health, 19,* 93–98.

White, M., Goldkamp, J., & Campbell, S. (2005). Beyond mandatory arrest: Developing a comprehensive response to domestic violence. *Police Practice and Research, 6,* 261–278.

Select Resources

- *Domestic Violence Awareness Project:* http://www.nrcdv.org/dvam/

- *Domestic Violence Prevention Enhancement and Leadership Through Alliances (DELTA):* http://www.cdc.gov/ncipc/DELTA/

- *How to Respond to Employees Facing Domestic Violence: A Workplace Handbook for Managers, Supervisors, and Co-Workers:* http://www.cambridgepublic health.org/publications/domestic-violence-workplace-booklet.pdf

- *Faith Trust Institute:* http://www.cpsdv.org/

- *MassLegalHelp:* http://www.masslegalhelp.org/domestic-violence/dom estic-violence-and-schools

- *Men Can Stop Rape:* http://www.mencanstoprape.org/

- *Men Stopping Violence:* http://www.menstoppingviolence.org/

- *National Center for Children Exposed to Violence:* http://www.nccev.org/ violence/domestic.html

- *PreventConnect.org:* http://www.preventconnect.org/display/dis playHome.cfm

- *VAWnet:* http://new.vawnet.org/category/Main_Doc.php?docid=837

Nine

Moving Forward: Yes, We Can Reduce Intimate Partner Violence

In this final chapter, I identify strategies that I believe are critical to addressing intimate partner violence. I hope that you will use this chapter to focus on developing your own plan of action at the individual, community, or policy levels. As you consider how to reduce intimate partner violence, start with the idea that it can be done. However, it takes more than just a knowledge of domestic violence, it also takes reflection on what is most important to you and one dedicated collective response for change. As the field of social work moves forward, I believe it is important to understand our own issues, where we are, and how we use ourselves in the process of developing stronger, more effective strategies. As we also recognize our limitations, we must identify our strengths and build coalitions to work with others. Only by working together can we succeed in addressing this problem. Whether you are new to the field or have worked in the field for many years, you need to invest consistently in self-introspection so that you can be true to the cause. I believe five specific features or components of strategies are critical in reducing intimate partner violence and eliminating it in the lives of women and girls: (1) community and faith-based approaches, (2) healthy relationship education, (3) intersectional program strategies, (4) intergenerational approaches, and (5) culturally and developmentally proficient programs as part of solid practice.

Community and Faith-based Approaches

Community and faith-based organizations are critical to helping us find solutions to end domestic violence (Bent-Goodley & Fowler, 2006; Brown, 2008; Fortune, 2006; Gillum, Sullivan, & Bybee, 2006; Horne & Levitt, 2003; Knickmeyer, Levitt, & Horne, 2010; Levitt & Ware, 2006; Puchala, Paul, Kennedy, & Mehl-Madrona, 2010; Pyles, 2007; Skiff, Horwitz, LaRussa-Trott, Pearson, & Santiago, 2008; Ware, Levitt, & Bayer, 2003; Yick, 2008). Working in the natural and indigenous environment and in communities gives us access to people who may not always request services from formal systems and providers. It also provides access to people who need additional support. One of the main issues often identified, particularly among women of color, is delayed help seeking. Many women turn to their faith-based communities, friends, and informal networks before they turn to formal provider systems. When they do, the systems should be there. Working in the natural environment as a partner gives practitioners credibility within the community, allows for a greater exchange of ideas about what does and does not work, and helps the community take ownership of the issue of domestic violence in their community. Formal providers also have more accountability for finding solutions in the communities they serve. So, engaging faith- and community-based organizations allows practitioners to move toward reducing intimate partner violence in communities through coordinated partnerships in which each collaborator is valued for its perspective and ability to address issues from within its cultural and geographic reality. Practitioners must also recognize that community groups may not have full knowledge or appreciation of what domestic violence encompasses, so practitioners must provide education and support. Practitioners may not be from the community or well versed in the community's specific needs. They can obtain this information by taking the initiative, through self-exploration, and by working with the group to understand the community's unique experiences. In the next wave of the domestic violence movement, it is vital that practitioners find creative solutions to eradicate domestic violence by connecting with and honoring communities' indigenous practices and solutions. More must be done to identify healing practices and models of interventions within the community and support them. Providing education so that practitioners and clients can hear each other will benefit both practitioners and clients. As social work moves forward, healing practices and models of intervention must be a focus, recognizing that healing does not mean that the pain is gone forever but that it is instead managed, that a sense of peace is found, and that practitioners understand what to do when the pain emerges (Litton & Williams, 2006).

Healthy Relationship Education

Conducting healthy relationship education in concert with domestic violence prevention and intervention is critical. It is clear to me that practitioners cannot talk about the problem of domestic violence without advancing the conversation of what constitutes a healthy relationship. Many people are unclear as to what the characteristics of a healthy relationship are and whether one can be achieved. Domestic violence must be included as part of healthy relationship education curriculums (Pardue & Rector, 2004; Whiting, Bradford, Vail, Carlton, & Bathje, 2009). Most healthy relationship education programs do not or are reluctant to address domestic violence (Roberts, 2006). Yet half of couples seeking therapy have violence present in the relationship (Roberts, 2006). Practitioners must begin exposing young people and adults to what a healthy relationship looks like. Talking about healthy relationships also provides an opportunity to bring more people to the table. So often, negative perceptions and stigma are associated with talking about domestic violence because some people view it as being a negative and divisive issue; however, talking about healthy relationships is something that is valued in communities and does not have a stigma associated with it. Using healthy relationship education as an opportunity to talk to people about domestic violence prevention and intervention is an important strategy.

Practitioners have to look at healthy relationship education as an opportunity to do more than just talk about building strong communication skills and to provide strategies for managing conflict, self-exploration, development of healthy ideas of what it means to be a man and a woman dealing with anger, and building self-esteem. Healthy relationship education also provides an opportunity for mentorship by and models of couples in healthy relationships so that people can see that healthy relationships do exist and that they are possible. Healthy relationship curriculums that include domestic violence prevention messages are key. These programs cannot be offered without including awareness of and education on domestic violence prevention, identifying how to respond to domestic violence, and providing local resources that participants can access for assistance.

Intersectional Programs and Practices

It is critical that practitioners acknowledge that domestic violence is not an issue best addressed in isolation but that it intersects with many other health and social issues. Intersectional programs allow practitioners to address issues in a more comprehensive and holistic fashion. It allows them to address issues more effectively with a broader understanding of their complexity. Practitioners must still maintain a focus on domestic violence as its own issue; however, while focusing on developing and designing interventions specific to domestic violence prevention messaging, it is also imperative to create practices and programs that focus on the intersection of these major social issues. As practitioners examine the intersection of these issues, they must also continue to build interdisciplinary relationships with colleagues and others to address needs. Intersectional programs widen the impact of primary prevention efforts and allow for greater cross-collaboration among substantive areas.

Intergenerational Approaches

It is important to design services that speak to the multiple transitions from childhood into older adulthood. Using a life span or transition approach related to domestic violence is very important in addressing the cyclical nature of violence (Ehrensaft et al., 2003; Lieberman, 2007; Pollak, 2004; Purvin, 2003). As researchers design interventions, they have an opportunity to get to the root cause of intimate partner violence, prevent further violence in the family unit, create greater exchanges across generations, and build communication and learning opportunities. These exchanges create the opportunity to understand differing perspectives and realities and aid in fostering learning outside of formal agency program schedules. The exchange between mothers and daughters, grandmothers and granddaughters, fathers and daughters, and mothers and sons can be powerful. If supported and facilitated, these intergenerational, intergender dialogues can strengthen awareness of historical and cyclical family challenges and can uncover the resilience and ability to move forward. Thus, more time and energy are needed to discern how to best address this issue.

Culturally Proficient Practice

Being culturally proficient in service delivery must be viewed as good practice. Cultural competence should not be treated as something to check off or viewed as something else to do. It must be incorporated and integrated into practice in the same way as ethics, interpersonal skills, and interviewing skills. To address domestic violence most effectively, practitioners must provide services that are culturally and developmentally centered. They can no longer afford to provide services that are not respectful and understanding of the communities they serve. Culture goes far beyond the number of staff of color or documents in the community's language. There is nothing vague about culturally proficient practice. I always emphasize that cultural context is not simply developing an African dance program or translating a brochure in a domestic violence program; rather, it speaks to staffing patterns, board membership, programs and policies, community relationships, and strategies used in the agency. It speaks to the pictures on the wall, the services provided, and the philosophical thinking behind the organization's strategies and functioning. Cultural proficiency also means establishing relationships with the indigenous community; knowing indigenous practices; and having people, regardless of race or ethnic specificity, with the skill and mindset to fully engage and successfully work with indigenous populations. Practitioners must support indigenous communities in finding their own solutions to the problem of intimate partner violence and creating opportunities for them to empower themselves (Bent-Goodley, 2005, 2009; Hampton, LaTaillade, Dacey, & Marghi, 2008; Jones, 2008; Kallivay-alil, 2010; Montalvo-Liendo, 2009; Sumter, 2006; Tehee & Esqueda, 2008; Wallach, Weingram, & Avitan, 2010). People's culture must be respected and acknowledged for its strength and the resilience of its members. The community's historical relationship with the agency, formal providers, and others must be taken into account. Organizations and providers should be visible in the community, and their ability to meet the group's cultural needs should be transparent. Some think that social workers are not required to be culturally proficient. Conducting an assessment of your institution and your own practice is an important first step in examining the relevance and utility of your work and that of your organization. Letting community groups use evaluations to review and assess cultural proficiency can be helpful and provide a report card to the agency on its efficiency in the area. If you are not culturally proficient, then you are not engaging in good practice.

Role of Policy and Advocacy

It is critical that domestic violence programs maintain their focus on policy development and advocacy. So much of the work that social workers do focuses on individual and community work; however, it is imperative that they focus on the broader context of intimate partner violence. Social workers must continue to be advocates, no matter their role. Social workers must remember the value of their voices at the table and in the history of the domestic violence movement. If not for a courageous group of women willing to take a chance at change for thousands of women affected by this issue, the movement would not be where it is today. These women had the selflessness and courage to stand and voice the pain and silence of generations of women, and future generations must capture this selflessness and courage. It is critical that social work embrace this legacy and social work's role in continuing to advance the movement. Being an advocate does not mean that one will always or should always agree. In fact, it is through these diverse voices that practitioners are most powerful. Social work has to expand its focus to include the global agenda, addressing societal violence and latent messages in music and movies. It must further the message that violence is wrong and include new partnerships and allies to effect change.

Violence and Society

People cannot divorce the violence within the larger society from what they see in their homes. Again, practitioners need to continue to understand the societal context of violence and how it creates an environment that justifies the abuse of women and work toward change. They have to develop stronger partnerships with the entertainment industry and multimedia venues so that they can begin to have an impact on messages regarding women. NASW is doing important work with the entertainment industry to begin looking at messages sent about women and social work and to offer alternative, honest messages and promote more accurate critiques of social work practice and practice-related issues. As a profession, social work must support this initiative. Domestic violence advocates must form a coalition with like-minded groups to do similar work on domestic violence. Advocates also have to begin working with and support those who promote positive messages so as to counter the negative messages.

Coalition Building

Finally, I would like to emphasize the importance of building coalitions. Social workers cannot do this work alone. It requires coalitions of different people from different walks of life and different perspectives to come together as a single voice to say that violence is wrong and it must end (Malik, Ward, & Janczewski, 2008; Pennington-Zoellner, 2009; Salazar, Emshoff, Baker, & Crowley, 2007). Social workers must be able to work in partnership with others and, recognizing their strengths, limitations, and opportunities, bring ideas to the table that will allow them to address domestic violence most effectively. Despite funding challenges and scarce resources, organizations must work together and advocate for an increase in funding to widen the pool rather than fight for what is left.

Reflecting Pool

In this Reflecting Pool, I want to challenge you to develop your own plan of action and think about what you can do in your sphere of influence. I have explored some strategies to consider as the profession moves forward, but consider what this means for you, where you are, and your next steps.

My Reflection

I continue to be asked, "Why domestic violence? Why are you so interested in this area?" The simplest response is that domestic violence is wrong, and we have the power to do something about it. Fundamentally, I believe that domestic violence is one of the most violating forms of oppression because it can create self-doubt and pain for generations of families and within communities. It is unjust, unnecessary, and has the potential to be solved. My ability to do this work is fueled by a desire for change and because I have seen the resilience and strength of women who have been able to transcend the violence. I have seen children lead positive and productive lives even after witnessing abuse. So, I know about the power of possibility. I also recognize that it takes a collective response to address this issue. In recent years, I have increased my partnerships with men, fatherhood organizations, and faith-based groups to find and develop solutions that are sustainable and centered in transformation and healing. I strongly believe that to combat and eventually eradicate intimate partner violence, we must be willing to work together to find solutions that make sense for people regardless of who they are, where they come from, or how they present themselves. In the end, we have the collective power to eradicate intimate partner violence.

Your Reflection

- What next steps can you take to create change regarding domestic violence?
- Who should be at the table?
- What are your strengths and limitations?
- Who do you need to connect with so that you can be a better and more effective provider in this area?
- Do you require additional training?
- Do you have the appropriate supervision and consultation?

Notes:

_____
_____
_____
_____
_____
_____
_____
_____
_____
_____
_____
_____
_____
_____
_____
_____
_____
_____

Domestic Violence Action Plan

What do I need to do to advance my knowledge, attitude, and skills related to domestic violence?	
Knowledge:	
Attitude:	
Skills:	
How do I strengthen my awareness of diversity as it relates to domestic violence?	
Self-knowledge:	
Knowledge of population(s):	
Skills needed:	
What myths or stereotypes do I have that could affect my ability to do my best work in this area?	
Myths:	
Stereotypes:	
Note. With whom do I consult to answer this question? How did I arrive at this response?	
What specific steps can I take to provide more efficient domestic violence services?	
Individual level:	
Agency or institutional level:	
Community level:	
How can I participate in advocacy issues?	
Local:	
State:	
National:	
International:	
Other action items:	
Note. Consider other action items that you can use to advance domestic violence prevention and intervention efforts.	

References

Bent-Goodley, T. B. (2005). An African-centered approach to domestic violence. *Families in Society, 86,* 197–206.

Bent-Goodley, T. B. (2009). A black experience–based approach to gender-based violence. *Social Work, 54,* 262–269.

Bent-Goodley, T. B., & Fowler, D. (2006). Spiritual and religious abuse. *Affilia: Journal of Women and Social Work, 21,* 282–295.

Brown, M. (2008, April). The politics of faith in domestic violence programs. Paper presented at the annual meeting of the Midwestern Political Science Association Annual National Conference, Chicago.

Ehrensaft, M., Cohen, P., Brown, J., Smailes, E., Chen, H., & Johnson, J. (2003). Intergenerational transmission of partner violence: A 20–year prospective study. *Journal of Consulting and Clinical Psychology, 71,* 741–753.

Fortune, M. (2006). National declaration of religious and spiritual leaders addressing violence against women. *Journal of Religion & Abuse, 8,* 71–77.

Gillum, T., Sullivan, C., & Bybee, D. (2006). The importance of spirituality in the lives of domestic violence survivors. *Violence Against Women, 12,* 240–250.

Hampton, R., LaTaillade, J., Dacey, A., & Marghi, J. (2008). Evaluating domestic violence interventions for black women. *Journal of Aggression, Maltreatment & Trauma, 16,* 330–353.

Horne, S., & Levitt, H. (2003). Shelter from the raging wind: Religious needs of victims of intimate partner violence and faith leaders' responses. *Journal of Religion & Abuse, 5,* 83–97.

Jones, L. (2008). The distinctive characteristics and needs of domestic violence victims in a Native American community. *Journal of Family Violence, 23,* 113–118.

Kallivayalil, D. (2010). Narratives of suffering of South Asian immigrant survivors of domestic violence. *Violence Against Women, 16,* 789–811.

Knickmeyer, N., Levitt, H., & Horne, S. (2010). Putting on Sunday best: The silencing of battered women within Christian faith communities. *Feminism & Psychology, 20,* 94–113.

Levitt, H., & Ware, K. (2006). "Anything with two heads is a monster": Religious leaders' perspectives on marital equality and domestic violence. *Violence Against Women, 12,* 1169–1190.

Lieberman, A. (2007). Ghosts and angels: Intergenerational patterns in the transmission and treatment of the traumatic sequelae of domestic violence. *Infant Mental Health Journal, 28,* 422–439.

Litton, L., & Williams, O. (2006). *Ozha Wahbegannis: Exploring supervised visitation and exchange services in Native American communities.* St. Paul, MN: Institute on Domestic Violence in the African American Community.

Malik, N., Ward, K., & Janczewski, C. (2008). Coordinated community response to family violence: The role of domestic violence service organizations. *Journal of Interpersonal Violence, 23,* 933–955.

Montalvo-Liendo, N. (2009). Cross-cultural factors in disclosure of intimate partner violence: An integrated review. *Journal of Advanced Nursing, 65,* 20–34.

Pardue, M., & Rector, R. (2004). *Reducing domestic violence: How the healthy marriage initiative can help* (Backgrounder 1744). Washington, DC: Heritage Foundation.

Pennington-Zoellner, K. (2009). Expanding "community" in the community response to intimate partner violence. *Journal of Family Violence, 24,* 539–545.

Pollak, R. (2004). An intergenerational model of domestic violence. *Journal of Population Economics, 17,* 311–329.

Puchala, C., Paul, S., Kennedy, C., & Mehl-Madrona, L. (2010). Using traditional spirituality to reduce domestic violence within Aboriginal communities. *Journal of Alternative and Complementary Medicine, 16,* 89–96.

Purvin, D. (2003). Weaving a triangled safety net: The intergenerational legacy of domestic violence and poverty. *Violence Against Women, 9,* 1263–1277.

Pyles, L. (2007). The complexities of the religious response to domestic violence: Implications for faith-based initiatives. *Affilia: Journal of Women and Social Work, 22,* 281–291.

Roberts, P. (2006). *Building bridges between the healthy marriage, responsible fatherhood and domestic violence movements: Issues, concerns and recommendations* (Policy Brief 7). Washington, DC: Center for Law and Social Policy.

Salazar, L., Emshoff, J., Baker, C., & Crowley, T. (2007). Examining the behavior of a system: An outcome evaluation of a coordinated community response to domestic violence. *Journal of Family Violence, 22,* 631–641.

Skiff, D., Horwitz, S., LaRussa-Trott, M., Pearson, J., & Santiago, L. (2008). Engaging the clergy in addressing the impact of partner violence in their faith communities. *Journal of Spirituality in Mental Health, 10,* 101–118.

Sumter, M. (2006). Domestic violence and diversity: A call for multicultural services. *Journal of Health & Human Services Administration, 29,* 173–190.

Tehee, M., & Esqueda, C. (2008). American Indian and European American women's perceptions of domestic violence. *Journal of Family Violence, 23,* 25–35.

Wallach, H., Weingram, Z., & Avitan, O. (2010). Attitudes toward domestic violence: A cultural perspective. *Journal of Interpersonal Violence, 25,* 1284–1297.

Ware, K., Levitt, H., & Bayer, G. (2003). May God help you: Faith leaders' perspectives of intimate partner violence within their communities. *Journal of Religion & Abuse, 5,* 55–81.

Whiting, J., Bradford, K., Vail, A., Carlton, E., & Bathje, K. (2009). Developing a domestic violence protocol for marriage education: Critical components and outcomes. *Journal of Couple and Relationship Therapy, 8,* 181–196.

Yick, A. (2008). A metasynthesis of qualitative findings on the role of spirituality and religiosity among culturally diverse domestic violence survivors. *Qualitative Health Research, 18,* 1289–1306.

Resources

- *The Advocates for Human Rights:* http://stopvaw.org/domestic_violence_training_modules.html

- *Avon Foundation:* http://info.avonfoundation.org/site/PageServer?pagename=wtc_home

- *Institute on Violence, Abuse and Trauma:* http://www.ivatcenters.org/

- *Family Justice Centers Alliance:* http://www.familyjusticecenter.com/

- *Family Violence Prevention Fund Campaigns:* http://www.endabuse.org/section/campaigns/

- *Mary Kay:* http://www.businesswire.com/smp/MaryKay-Domestic Violence-SurveyAndPlan/

- *Men Can Stop Rape:* http://www.mencanstoprape.org/

- *National Center on Domestic and Sexual Violence Advocacy Groups:* http://www.ncdsv.org/ncd_linksadvoc.html

- *National Coalition Against Domestic Violence:* http://www.ncadv.org/

- *National Family Violence Legislative Resource Center:* http://www.nfvlrc.org/

- *PreventConnect.org:* http://www.preventconnect.org/display/displayHome.cfm

- *Verizon Wireless:* http://aboutus.vzw.com/communityservice/hopeLine.html

- *Women of Color Network:* http://womenofcolornetwork.org/

- *Women of Color United:* http://www.womenofcolorunited.org/about-women-of-color-united/

Index

Index

Montminy, L., 7
Moon, S., 62
Moore, S., 168
Moracco, K. E., 8
Morales-Aleman, M. M., 96
Morgan, K., 49
Morrill, A., 140
mothers, protection of children by, 92
Motivans, M., 5
Mourad, M., 98
Mucci, I., 115, 116
Mullen, E. J., 152
murders and substance abuse, 90
murders of men, 5
murders of women
    pregnancy and, 94–95
    risks factors, 5, 73–76
    statistics, 3, 4
    suicides and, 5
    teens and, 114
Murphy, C. M., 14, 61, 62
Musgrave, C. F., 38
myths and domestic violence, 39–43

Nachimson, D., 97
narcissistic personality disorder and
    perpetrators, 132
Nason-Clark, N., 61
NASW standards on cultural competency,
    18–19
National Association of Social Workers
    (2001), 18–19
National Association of Social Workers
    (2008), 76
National Campaign to Prevent Teen
    and Unplanned Pregnancy and
    CosmoGirl.com (2008), 114
National Center for Injury Control and
    Prevention (2005), 118
National Center for Injury Prevention and
    Control (2003), 4, 56
National Crime Victimization Survey, 3–4

National Domestic Violence Hotline, 82, 83
National Incident Based Reporting
    System, 166
National Institute of Justice (2010), 12
National Network to End Domestic
    Violence (2009), 4, 91
Native Americans, 12–13, 17, 42
Nedd, D., 12
neglect, educational, 91
Nelms, A. P., 96
Nelson, D., 94
Newlove, T., 32
Newman, F., 7
Nguyen, T., 135
Nixon, J., 7
Noonan, R., 116
Norris, F., 4
notification of perpetrator release from
    prison, 100
Nuttall, R., 95

O'Campo, B., 118
O'Campo, P., 94
O'Dell, A., 166
Oehme, K., 140, 141
Office of Juvenile Justice and Delinquency
    Prevention, 170
Okamura, A., 16, 17
O'Keefe, M., 114
O'Leary, A., 96
O'Leary, D., 33
Oliver, W., 100, 135, 137
Oomen-Early, J., 17
oppression, domestic violence as, 188
oppression, historical experiences of, 12
oppression, intersectionality of, 13, 37
oral health, connection to domestic
    violence of, 95–96
Orloff, L., 16
Ornduff, S. R., 33
Ortega, D., 92
Osborne, B., 97

__ Index __